GOD WHISPERED
"I'VE GOT THIS"

FuzionPress

My true story walks the glorious peaks and the dark and often hopeless valleys of this thing called life.

~Trudy Bondhus Lohre

GOD WHISPERED
"I'VE GOT THIS"

A FAITH-BASED BOOK FOR CAREGIVERS

TRUDY BONDHUS LOHRE

First Printing: August 2023
First Edition

Paperback ISBN: 978-1-955541-21-3
eBook ISBN: 978-1-955541-22-0
Hardcover ISBN: 978-1-955541-23-7
LCCN:

Cover and interior design by Ann Aubitz
Cover photo by Trudy Bondhus Lohre

Published by FuzionPress
1250 E 115th Street
Burnsville, MN 55337
Fuzionpress.com
612-781-2815

This book is dedicated to
God for helping make this book possible
To Jim, who endured so much but chose to
live by faith and God's grace
To my dear friends and family, who gave
immeasurable support
To my beloved children, who have stood by my side
To Ann for believing in me

TABLE OF CONTENTS

INTRODUCTION

This book is a documentary of my real-life journey where I share the overwhelming health struggles that life handed us. Everyone faces challenges in life in some form. Ours were primarily health-related and encompassed everything from an organ transplant to several types of cancer and other major health obstacles along the way. Throughout my journey, I have shared personal stories as a caregiver for my loved one. Equally as important, I shared scriptures and stories that have brought me to this day. I struggled and questioned God for allowing this much pain. I lost my faith only to find it had returned even stronger than before.

Life is difficult, and no one on this earth is free from struggles. But through our trials, a lifeline is waiting if we simply accept. It's our choice, and no one can make it for us.

Lastly, I write this book as a tribute to my life partner, Jim. As you read further along in the book, I sincerely hope you are genuinely inspired by how this man reacted to what he had to endure. Each time he survived; he would then face a new challenge waiting to threaten his life. His undying determination and faith were God inspired. He humbly was unaware of how his life illustrated the power of faith to others.

We live in a troubled world where it only worsens as each day passes. Whenever we turn on the news, we question where life is headed. If you are looking for hope and direction in your personal life—I genuinely believe this book will help you in your journey, no matter your struggles. My prayer is that it does.

THE FOURTH QUARTER

I come from a sports family, so it is easy to compare my life to the game of basketball. I am in the fourth and final quarter of the game. Hopefully, I'm not near the final buzzer, but I must be honest the clock is ticking. But in the game of life, I realize that age is a sign of success and survival. When you look at the world around us now, it should be worn as a badge of honor if you have made it this far. You are still a player in the game. I now wear my scars and my age as signs of what I have overcome in life. I celebrate that I am a survivor, and I am proud of that fact, especially at my age. There are many people throughout our lives that are not fortunate to make it to their fourth quarter golden years. Whether it be illness, tragedy, or otherwise—they have made the journey to heaven earlier than most. Those left behind on this earth mourn their loss but have a guardian angel to walk beside them until they meet again.

So, here's the deal—I have survived seventy-one years on this earth, and I say that with a thankful heart. That makes me a senior citizen, a baby boomer, a bingo-playing old lady, a thrift store shopper, and someone fast approaching US citizens' average life expectancy! I tell you this for one reason only. I have made it this far because of God. Without His guidance, protection, and love, I would not be here today. He is the reason I am still here on this earth. My work is unfinished, and this book may be part of God's divine plan for me at this moment in my life.

I lived my life for many years, thinking my faith was where it needed to be. But as I look back over the past twenty-plus years, a bird's eye view of my faith sliding scale would resemble a thermometer in Minnesota during April. We can go from a snowstorm to a thunderstorm to a heat wave all in a matter of days. I am not proud of how my faith bounced around, but I am just being honest. The surprising realization is that I always thought my faith was strong. But I know now I was mistaken. I believed in God but fell short because I did not draw from His strength, peace, and unending love like I could and should have. I didn't understand the depth of what He could provide, and because of this, it caused me undue anguish. As each chapter of my journey progressed, I became more and more aware of the indescribable strength the Lord can provide. My faith has become increasingly reliant on God's loving arms, and He is my protector.

It amazes me how as humans, we think we are in control. The truth is we can really mess things up when we go it alone. But if we genuinely believe in our soul, the lifeline of "Let Go and Let God," we will not have to go it alone. God never promised us a life with no trials or troubles. But He did promise to walk by our side through our trials each step of the way. Each life walk strengthens us and helps us realize how thankful we should be for all the good times. Being thankful for the blessings in life pleases God and better prepares us for the next trial that He will guide us through if we just let Him.

About a year ago, I read a bible verse that helped me understand my faith journey for so long. This verse will again be referenced later, bringing even more light to my story. The verse was from Psalm 32:7 NIV, "You are my hiding place. You will protect me from trouble and surround me with songs of deliverance." Note it doesn't say that we will never experience trouble —but rather that we will be protected while enduring our troubles. This verse gives us hope that God is always there by our side, whatever life throws at us. We can find solace and comfort in His hiding place, which I interpret as our time of prayer spent with Him.

As Psalm 23:4 tells us, "Even though I walk through the valley of the shadow of death, I will fear no evil for you are with me; your rod and your staff, they comfort me." Our faith walk is neither perfect nor easy, but I believe each bend in the road is there for a purpose. We can choose to walk this life by our own strength, but my sincere hope is that this book will help you realize what I have realized. We have so much strength available at our disposal from our Lord and Savior. We need to ask for His help while thanking Him for the blessings right in front of our eyes. Doing so will make our journey on earth much more enjoyable. It will be easier to handle the hard times and have eternal outcomes we could not achieve alone.

Sadly, I lived so many years without realizing this and trying to go it alone. But now, at my age, I have survived trials, battles, and disappointments, and I proudly wear the scars from each. I have learned that I am not in this alone. This endeavor of writing a book has been on my mind for several years. I always felt I would fall short, and it wouldn't happen. Also, with each passing year, my life kept adding more and more chapters to my unwritten book. How could I possibly write everything I had faced, let alone have people want to read my journey? But months ago, it was as if God spoke to me. I had an overwhelming feeling that if I asked for His help with every word I wrote, maybe my book could become a reality. But given that I am in the fourth and final quarter of my life, I figured I needed to get off the bench and start playing. With God's help, I needed to begin writing now to beat the final buzzer. None of us know how much time we have left, but I have a story to tell that I believe could help you through your journey. I pray that you enjoy my writings, and the pages will bring you hope, comfort, and God's peace in whatever life has thrown your way. As you read my book, I hope you realize that we all fall short. But remember, God never says, "Okay, you keep messing up, and I'm done with you." He never gives up on us. Never.

DON'T GIVE ME ANYMORE TO HANDLE

My book begins with a new chapter in my life. After my divorce, I remained in my home state of Minnesota for a year until moving in August of 2000 to Pennsylvania. My uncle had invited me, and I took him up on the offer at a time when my future was uncertain. After returning to Minnesota the following year, I moved to Arizona in August 2002. My move was for reasons any mama would understand. It was a very trying and incredibly lonely time for me. My "mission" was to save my daughter. She had fallen into the wicked world of drugs and lived a very dark life. I was naive enough to think I would move across the country, show up and offer support, and she would be able to leave that world behind. Little did I know that this evil would have its' hold on her so tight that her mother's love didn't stand a chance. Satan had his grip and wouldn't let go. He loved that our family was broken and celebrated every time the drugs won the battle with her inner self.

From Labor Day to November 8, I cried myself to sleep most nights. I really cannot express in words the despair and helplessness I felt. I had left my home back in Minnesota, including my job, friends, family, and Jim—to save my daughter. I would repeatably get her late-night phone calls saying to please come get her. She said she was ready to leave her world behind. After driving forty-five minutes in the middle of the night, I would get to her apartment, and one of two scenarios would play out. Either A, she would have passed out, or B, she would refuse to come with me and yell at me to stay out of her business. I would turn around, go to my truck, and drive back to my apartment. I remember sobbing so hard I could barely see the highway.

Looking back at 2002 and how I prayed to God, I realize I was not near as far on my faith journey as I thought. I prayed repeatedly that she would give up evil and come home. I spent endless nights lying awake and consumed with worry. I became so depressed and couldn't understand why my prayers weren't being answered. Each time she reached out, I would get my hopes up, only to have it all come crashing down again. It drove me more and more to a very dark place and pleading with God to rescue us both. I realize now that I kept asking God for an outcome I had chosen and never once turned it over to Him. My prayers were always my will and not His will.

This period in my life is when I began journaling. It helped to write my feelings down on paper, although it did not change the outcome. But when I needed it most, my writing became my therapy during such difficult times. This "personal therapy" stuck with me, and I have journaled ever since. My journal writings and vivid memories have been an essential resource for my book. Reading many of my entries was painful, but there were also times to be celebrated. Looking back at this period of my life, I would do it all over again. A mother's love is deep, and I tried with all my power to help my daughter find her way.

On the evening of November 8, 2002, I remember praying to God before falling asleep. I was distraught, almost to the point of anger. I pleaded with God to NOT give me anymore to handle. I felt so alone at that moment and felt like I couldn't do this anymore. I drifted off to sleep, only to be awakened around 12:30 a.m. by a phone call from my brother, Wayne, back home in Minnesota. I could hear the seriousness in his voice. He told me that our mother had just died from a heart attack. I was completely shocked and immediately reflected on my prayer only a few hours earlier. I was angry and had pleaded to God for nothing more to handle, and now I had just gotten the news my mom passed away. My first thoughts were, "Where are you, God? How could you do this to me?" I was in disbelief as I had just spoken with her twelve hours before. She had just gotten discharged from the hospital that afternoon and was back home again with my dad. How could this even happen?

Numb, still angry, and in a robot manner, I booked a one-way flight from Arizona back home to Minnesota. At the airport, because this was only one year after 9/11, all one-way flights were treated suspiciously, especially those purchased just hours earlier. I was searched, and the entire contents of my suitcase were emptied onto a large table. After agents rummaged through everything in my luggage, I was approved to board, and the agents walked away. I was left alone standing there to re-pack my suitcase and hurriedly make my way to the gate before my plane departed. The most painful memory of my airport experience was the pit in my stomach, and I thought I would vomit. Looking back, I felt so alone; my biggest mistake was thinking

I was in charge. My strongest emotion was a feeling of anger toward God. I now so regret not reaching out for His lifeline. It would not have brought my mom back or helped to heal me right then and there. But it would have given me strength and comfort to handle what lies ahead.

The bible verse I should have turned to is Proverbs 3:5-6, "Trust in the Lord with all your heart and lean not on your own understanding; in all your ways acknowledge him, and he will make your paths straight." Referring once again to Psalm 32:7, He does not keep us from trouble but protects us through our trouble. He is always there waiting for us to reach out. Always. Looking back now, it is clear to me that the faith I had back then was in its infancy. Despite being fifty years old at the time, I had so much to learn. I grew up in a Christian home. I had always believed in God and thought I was right where I needed to be in my Christian journey. Little did I know how wrong I was and how much I needed God at every turn. This book depicts my faith journey, and you will see how God protected me throughout each and every struggle. And trust me; it seemed every time I turned around, trouble was staring me in the face. I experienced many emotions ranging from anger, hurt, loneliness, gratitude, and thankfulness. Over time, I finally shed the idea that I could do this thing called 'life" alone. As in the game of basketball, I was throwing up three-pointers, and every one missed the mark. Eventually, I saw the light, and my faith grew to a new level. I thank God every day for not giving up on me. As Psalm 32:7 states, "God surrounded me with songs of deliverance." Don't get me wrong. I have never finished my faith walk nor feel I am where I need to be. This isn't a journey where we one day wake up and say, "I think I've done all I can, and my faith has reached my definition of perfection." No, this is an ongoing partnership with God, and it needs daily nourishment to survive. We will be working towards perfection right up until our final breath.

MY FAITH THERMOMETER

Each chapter of my life brought new challenges and victories and moved me along the sliding thermometer of my Christianity. Thermometers are used to measure several things. First, there is the thermometer that takes our temperature. We are all most familiar with this one and turn to it when not feeling well. It gives us a snapshot of our overall health and when we need medical attention.

Another example is the thermometer used by fundraisers. This is used to measure how far they have come towards meeting their financial goal. It is a gauge for when they need to step things up and incorporate the help of others to reach their mission.

My thermometer is an indicator as well. It measures where I am on my faith walk with God. Obviously, the goal would be to always be near the top. But as humans, we slide, and only by the grace of God does He help us move the needle back upwards. One important thing I have learned is that we alone *cannot* keep the needle towards the top. We need daily guidance from God and must earnestly engage with Him for His help. Our Lord and

Savior was crucified and died on the cross for our sins. Our debt has been paid; all we need to do is reach out to Him. It is free and is right in front of our faces. We need to ask.

Earlier in my life, I thought I was near the top of the sliding scale or thermometer. This is where our faith is perfect and strong. But I discovered at each life event I was nowhere near the top. It has taken me a lifetime to move the needle, ever so slowly but steadily, up this thermometer. As humans, our scale can and probably will backslide when we meet life's challenges. This is when it is critical to turn our hearts to God at these times. We need to ask for His forgiveness for our doubt, as well as asking for His help. This crucial step in our faith will at least minimize the needle's backsliding. Because we are all human, while on this earth, it will be impossible for us to reach the very top of the thermometer. Jesus, our Lord, is the only one who has achieved this honor. That is perfect faith, and it only belongs to Him.

But we must strive daily to stay focused and do our best not to let the needle spiral downwards. But if it does, we must first recognize it and pray for God's help to get back on track. If we don't do this, we will find ourselves moving closer and closer to the bottom. If we allow ourselves to remain there long enough, we risk losing our grip and falling completely off the scale. This is a dark place and one where Satan celebrates our residency. He will do all in his power to keep us there. But thankfully, Satan is no match for God.

We need to keep trying every single day. It is the least we can do to honor the sacrifice God gave us with his son, Jesus, on the cross. If we genuinely want to get out of the deep dark hole and allow God to help us find our way back—He will throw us a lifeline, and we need to hold on with all our strength. The question is NOT if God will let go of the lifeline, but if we let go. So, hold on for dear life, and you will be back on track with God's help. Once again, He will be by your side to help move the needle upwards again. As I mentioned earlier, there will be times in your life when your thermometer may look like it's measuring a Minnesota weather pattern. It could be eighty degrees one day and fifty the next. It could be storming in the morning and beautiful sunshine with a rainbow by early afternoon. Or it could resemble an early spring snowstorm with puddles by the next day. This is called life; our challenge is recognizing that we can't walk alone. We have a lifeline available to us 24/7.

God never promises a life surrounded by a bed of roses, but He does promise to walk by your side every minute of every day. We always make huge mistakes, including myself, thinking that we know what is best for us. It could be something as simple as a red traffic light. We get disgusted that we didn't make the green light and must pause despite being in a hurry. But we do not get to see the future. Possibly just ahead, a driver will run a red light or suffer a medical emergency. By us stopping for our red light—He provided protection from a severe accident that we never even knew we needed.

I believe God sends these divine interventions on a daily basis. But unfortunately, we are usually too busy or distracted to notice. But He still sends them anyway. As humans, we view these as annoying detractors to our busy lives. But I can only imagine that He is just waiting for the day we stop and realize what He is doing for us behind the scenes. Everything that happens in our life is planned, and we need to trust that He knows what is best for us. Trust me, we sure as heck don't know! We are bummed when we don't make the green light, or our team doesn't make the playoffs. (If you are from Minnesota—you can relate!) Or, more seriously, if we don't get the promotion, if a relationship doesn't work out the way we had hoped, if we become seriously ill despite taking good care of our body—we become discouraged and think we are in this alone. The list goes on and on, depicting what life will throw our way. So, ask yourself if you would rather walk it alone or with God's protecting arms around you at every turn.

Back to the thermometer, when one does fall toward the bottom, sadly, it may be for a day, a week, or even a month or more. If Satan has his way, it can last years. The key to success starts with us. Seek out the Lord with all your heart, repent earnestly, and be willing to leave the dark hole behind. This is where He extends His hand and walks side by side with us. But this journey needs to be nourished daily with prayer and thanksgiving.

I have compared my faith journey to my car's gas tank. The empty side of the gas gauge is similar to the bottom of our "faith thermometer." We fear being stranded alongside the road when we drive close to empty. Nothing we can do here will fix this. It will take a call to AAA, and they will bring a lifeline in the form of a gas canister.

In the same way, our Lord becomes our lifeline and delivers us when our spiritual tank is empty. When we have a full gas tank, we drive our car confidently and don't worry about the low fuel light. But obviously, as we drive, we understand we must stop and refuel to keep going. The car doesn't do this automatically; we must make it happen. The same goes for our daily walk with the Lord. While a car can go days on a gas tank, our spiritual tank cannot. Our tank needs refueling daily, and God is there just waiting for us to ask.

As you read further in my book, you will discover time and time again how important it was for me to begin refueling my spiritual tank every day. This gives us the "gas" to make it through all the world throws at us. Equally important is to refuel again at the end of the day. My personal refueling consists of thanking God for walking alongside me throughout the day. I then list and thank God for all my blessings. This is a refueling that sadly can often get overlooked. I nightly thank Him for family members, naming each one. I began listing my children by name years ago and thanking God for them every day of my life. I remember watching them get on the school bus, and I would pray for God to protect them from harm, danger, and evil. I prayed for their health, happiness, comfort, and healing. The last two are key components of my prayers. Things will not always go our way in life, and we need God's healing help to get through the tough times. To this day, I speak this prayer every morning and every evening for my children.

I thank Him for the indescribable beauty of the sunset. I thank Him by naming my special friends, who are indeed a blessing to me. I thank Him for sending a cardinal to let me know my angel is watching over me. I thank Him for the serenity of the deer that gather in my backyard. I will even thank Him for something as simple as my favorite pillow to help me have a peaceful night's rest. I firmly believe with all my heart this refueling will change your life. Please give it a try. I have found that this is far more successful than simply praying to God and giving him our wish list. We need to pray, giving Him our sincere thanksgiving for our blessings and where we need His help. A picture in my room sums up so well how we should view our life on Earth. It simply states, "Write your hurts in the sand. Carve your blessings in stone."

But I know that when my time on earth is done, the Lord will move my faith needle on its' final journey to the top of my thermometer. This is our gift from God as we enter our heavenly home. I pray that everyone reading my book asks God for His help at every turn. This simple step will help prevent constant backsliding toward the bottom and allow God to help you strive toward the top. Life is much better there; you can see what your faith can accomplish. I finally understand what it means to truly "Let Go and Let God." It took me a while, but God never gave up on me. And for that, I thank Him.

BACK HOME AGAIN

A few weeks after my mother's funeral, Jim drove me back to Arizona. He had become a tower of strength for me. He always listened earnestly while I poured out my heart and was a comfort to me when I needed it most. Being away from my Minnesota family was difficult, but I felt compelled to return to Arizona. It was one of the best decisions I could have made. It took tough love—one of the most difficult challenges a parent will ever face. But with what I know now, divine intervention helped my daughter agree to enter a faith-based rehabilitation center. It was precisely where she needed to be, and Jim and I were with her every step of the way. We attended every session and told her that neither we nor God had forsaken her. Her father also flew out for a visit and offered his love and support on her journey. The following years weren't always easy, but she remained strong and promised herself and God to remain drug-free. I am so very proud of her and so very thankful. She has grown in her faith and has become an amazing and highly successful woman today because of her determination and God's grace. I will forever be grateful for this.

While living in Phoenix, Arizona, I met some incredible people. I worked for OfficeMax and then later went to work for Cabela's in Glendale. I had the privilege of working alongside some wonderful people who were like family. They meant the world to me while living away from my Minnesota home. To this day, I remain in touch with several of my co-workers and some great friends. Many of these great people still call me "mom." I sincerely hope they know how much they positively impacted my life. I hesitate to list their names because I know I will leave someone out. But I hope they know who they are and how grateful I am for each one.

In a few years, Jim joined me permanently in Arizona. Before that, he worked on road construction during the summers in Minnesota. He worked in New London for a family trucking business. They originally were from my hometown in SW Minnesota, and we even shared the same little white country church years ago. Now with Jim living in Phoenix year-round, he went to work for a large trucking business doing road construction. They had Minnesota ties and hired him on the spot when they saw where he had lived before his move to Arizona. They told him the Midwest had impressive work ethics and wanted him on their team. Their road construction business had built much of the freeway system in Phoenix. Jim drove a belly dump truck and occasionally would pull a double belly dump. He was a hard worker, and I always felt bad for him during the summers. The Arizona temps would reach 115 degrees, and hot asphalt couldn't have been a fun job! But I never heard him complain— he always said he was just thankful to be working.

A fun memory for me from our Arizona days happened in 2005. We attended Spirit of Joy—a wonderful church that warmly welcomed us. Pastor Dave was amazing and impacted both of our lives. The church was in Gilbert, and they wished to participate in the city-wide celebration. Gilbert Days hosted a parade, and the choir wanted to be included. The problem was they didn't have a truck big enough to fit the members and all the musical equipment. Jim asked his boss if he could borrow a semi and flatbed trailer. They graciously agreed, and the entire choir rode in the parade while Jim and I rode in the truck cab. Pastor Dave and his wife had a small daughter, and she rode in the truck with us as her mom and dad walked alongside the choir. I will never forget the pride that Jim had that day when he could help the church that had helped welcome us.

Fast forward to August 2007, when we decided to return home to Minnesota. My dad, whom I loved very much, was so lonely and never got over losing Mom in 2002. In addition, I had a son and brothers who lived in Minnesota. Sadly, one of my brothers was now suffering from lung cancer, Because of everything, I felt it was time to go back home. My other son and daughter, who lived in Phoenix, were doing well and I felt confident in returning to Minnesota. They knew I would keep them in my prayers. Plus, I knew my children would have my mother as their guardian angel to help them through life. Jim's family was also back in Minnesota, and it now seemed the right time to return home. I was a manager for Cabela's in Glendale and was fortunate to transfer back to Minnesota, where I would work at their Rogers, MN, location. So, we left my daughter, son, and many wonderful friends from our work and church family behind in Arizona.

After we got settled back in Minnesota, I began working at Cabela's in September 2007. Jim was hired shortly after to work there as well. We were blessed again at work to develop so many strong friendships. We became family and little did I know how much I would need them down the road. We also were blessed to have some incredible neighbors. I remember having great neighbors years ago when living in my hometown. And now, years later, I had found great neighbors once again. Their names are Bill and Karen; they were angels sent from above. We lived in a remote country setting, and they lived about half a mile down the road. They became such an essential part of our life. To this day, I am so grateful for their kindness, support, and always being there for us. I know God put them in our lives, knowing we would need them. I didn't know how much.

Looking back, I truly see God's hand at work over the years. My divorce was a painful time, as well as when I first moved to Arizona. But God led me to some amazing people I would never have met otherwise. These people would later become crucial to our lives and help us through unbelievable trials. God has a purpose for everything we go through, and it is not for us to try and understand. I am so grateful for His guiding hand, which led us to each and every one of these wonderful people who shared our journey. They are as much a part of our story as we are, and I am still so richly blessed by them.

BUCKLE UP—IT'S GOING TO GET BUMPY

This is the portion in my book where I will demonstrate how my faith got me through the next twelve years. The chapters ahead will spell out times when life was incredibly dark. But it will also tell of times when God would step in and miracles would happen. I previously spoke of the faith thermometer, and looking back, I realize my needle jumped around like a two-year-old who just ate three candy bars and missed their nap. I had all I could do to keep it together and not allow Satan to plummet my needle off the bottom of my thermometer. It would have been easy to blame God and reject my faith. I could have been so angry and only demanded answers from God as to why this was happening—repeatedly, again and again. I know now that I would not have made it through what life was about to hand us if I didn't have faith. My faith is 100 percent what kept me going with each passing year. I want to be very clear that it wasn't the fact that I was so great and strong. It is quite the opposite. But it was the fact that God was always at my side to help me through each battle. We walked this journey together, and He alone made this possible. I cannot wait until the day we meet again, and I can personally thank Him for never giving up on me.

As this chapter title states, I need to warn you this is where you need to buckle up. I'm sure to some, this journey I am about to write will seem almost like fiction. You will ask yourself how one man could keep beating the odds repeatedly. Even more so, you will ask yourself how he could always keep the faith, never give up, and, just as astounding, never complain. We did it together with God's never-ending help, and here is our story.

***

Jim had faced heart issues long before I met him. Jim had hereditary heart health as his mother died from a heart attack at fifty-two. Jim's first heart attack was at thirty-two years of age. As he dug fence post holes in a country field near New London, MN, he felt chest pain and shortness of breath. He turned to his co-worker and said, "I think I'm having a heart attack!". After arriving at a local hospital, it was discovered that this initial attack injured some of the muscles in his heart. This would set the stage for a lifetime of heart disease. When Jim was forty, he had a quadruple heart bypass to repair all four major arteries. This would decrease heart attacks, but the damage had already been done. His heart muscle couldn't do a sufficient job of pumping the blood throughout his body. He experienced many more heart issues over the following years before we met.

Back in 2005, while living in Phoenix, Jim faced heart problems again. The doctors implanted a combination pacemaker and defibrillator to regulate his heartbeat. The combined unit would also shock the heart back into rhythm when the electrical signal became so erratic that the heart would stop contracting. After moving back to Minnesota approximately three years after this implant, Jim was admitted to the hospital when the defibrillator malfunctioned. We were in our Monticello country home's kitchen when Jim suddenly fell off the chair onto the floor. He had been eating a bowl of Froot Loops (don't judge...he liked them!), and I remember cereal flying everywhere in the kitchen. The defibrillator had, without any reason, shocked Jim multiple times. The only winner of this frightening experience was our dog, Gunner, who graciously helped us clean up the cereal! Once we arrived at the hospital, and while he was sitting on the exam table—the unit violently shocked him again, and he almost went backward onto the floor. It was quickly determined that the unit was faulty and needed to be replaced immediately. The surgery was performed, and Jim was back in business. It was revealed that some of these units across the country had malfunctioned and were also deemed defective. That would have been helpful information to have had earlier. But luckily, the unit only shocked Jim on two occasions before they could replace it with a new and much-improved model.

Now fast forward two years to the early evening of March 17, 2010. Jim was now sixty years of age and had been outside on our farm with our awesome German Shorthair, Gunner. They were the absolute best of buddies and went everywhere together. A pack of wild dogs attacked Gunner out behind our home just one week earlier. Jim went outside with his shotgun, scared the dogs away, and saved Gunner's life. Gunner had severe wounds and consequently had to wear the "cone of shame," a plastic collar around his neck to prevent him from licking the deep cuts and drainage tubes on his upper back and neck.

I was inside the house and was in the process of coloring my hair with one of those drug store box kits. Jim and Gunner had returned from outside and sat down in the den. I was walking through the den on my way to the bathroom to shower and rinse the hair dye. As I passed Jim's recliner, he stood up, turned to me, and said, "I'm going to die." I remember saying to him, "No, you're not!" He looked me in the eyes and repeated those four words. He fell back against the window, then turned and collapsed onto the floor at my feet. This entire scene happened in about fifteen seconds.

To this day, I cannot find the words to explain how I felt at that exact moment. I knew immediately that every second counted, and I didn't have time to be shocked, crippled with fear, or second-guess myself. I immediately began CPR while holding the landline phone with my ear to call 911. Gunner was all over Jim and wouldn't step away. I continued CPR, answering a million questions from the 911 operator and struggling to keep Gunner and his plastic cone from getting in my way. I finally became frustrated with the 911 operator and told her I needed to focus on CPR and not on trying to hold the house phone to my ear. I didn't hang up, but I did throw the phone across the room. The next fourteen minutes seemed like an eternity.

After about seven or eight minutes, I remember so very well thinking why I was still desperately trying to save him. There was no pulse, and there was no sign of life. But I didn't give up, and I prayed for strength. Doing CPR training on a plastic dummy in a health class is one thing. But doing CPR for fourteen minutes for a loved one is a different ballgame. Your emotions are so raw, and you have to keep it together. Adrenaline took over, and I didn't stop administering CPR until the ambulance reached our remote country home. When they walked in,

I remember saying how relieved I was to see them. I stopped the CPR, and they said, "No! Don't stop until we're ready to administer the paddles." It was only a few seconds later, but how tired one gets from CPR is astounding. I pray you never have to experience it yourself—either as the giver or the receiver.

They tried reviving his heart three times by shocking him and finally got a feeble pulse on the third try. They immediately loaded him into the ambulance and raced down our gravel driveway. I will never forget the feeling of standing there with Gunner, watching the lights shining in the darkness and hearing the sirens racing down the gravel road. I did not know if Jim was alive, brain dead, or gone. I didn't know if I would ever hear his voice again, see his mischievous smile or walk hand in hand through the woods.

I only needed to jump into the shower for one reason: I had to remove the hair dye. It was the fastest shower I'd ever taken, and I got dressed and drove (way over the speed limit) to the local hospital about ten miles away. I now had somewhat processed what happened, but I don't remember the drive. I did not know if Jim was alive—I just knew I had to get there.

WHAT-IF'S

When I arrived, he showed no signs of life but had a feeble pulse. They were moving quickly and rushing him outside to the helicopter pad. I walked alongside the stretcher and held his hand. I would have given anything for him to open his eyes or show me his smile. But he lay there lifeless as they lifted him into the helicopter. The pilot told me they were taking him to Abbott, and I should drive there as quickly as possible. I remember standing there alone and watching the helicopter fly off into the night sky. The feeling of helplessness was overwhelming. First, I had watched the flashing lights of the ambulance race down our country driveway a short while ago. Now I was watching the flashing lights of the Life Link helicopter racing through the night sky toward Minneapolis.

I ran into the hospital to get directions to Abbott Heart Hospital, where they transferred him. I had never been there before and was given a printed map of what roads to take. I drove there in complete shock, not knowing if Jim was alive. Before this, I had called his son to tell him what had happened. He and a friend were returning home from the cities that evening and immediately turned his car around and headed to Abbott. I hurriedly parked and ran into the emergency department, where I was sent upstairs to the ICU unit of the heart hospital. I walked through the doors, and a doctor met me in the hall near his room. It was then I found out Jim was still alive, and I had a glimmer of hope.

The doctor explained that Jim had suffered a massive cardiac arrest and was in the most critical condition imaginable. He said, "I need to be completely honest with you. We are giving him a 5 percent chance of survival. We are cooling his body temperature to ninety-two degrees to help prevent further damage to his organs, including his heart and brain." I stood there paralyzed. I realized at this point he was still alive, although his chances were incredibly slim.

From the time Jim had collapsed only hours earlier, to his ambulance ride to Monticello, to his airlift to Abbott, and to my emotional drive to downtown Minneapolis—I went through all that not knowing if he was alive. Now I got my answer, only to learn that it could change at any moment. I could not believe what had happened in the past two hours, and I just wanted to push a rewind button or wake up from this nightmare. This is one of the moments in my life where my faith thermometer dived. I asked God why...why did this happen to such a kind man who didn't deserve this. He had battled heart issues for nearly thirty years, and we finally thought his pacemaker/defibrillator would handle any issues thrown his way. But they weren't a match for a massive cardiac arrest.

Thoughts raced through my head. I asked myself so many "what-ifs." What if he hadn't just come inside only five minutes earlier? What if he suffered this cardiac arrest outside with Gunner while I was in the shower? What if after my shower, when I didn't see Jim in the house, I went looking outside for him? What if, after about seven minutes of CRP, I had given up and stopped instead of performing it for another seven minutes? What if I had gotten in the shower only a minute earlier, and he would have been all alone in the den with no one to help? So many "what-ifs," but clearly, God wasn't ready for him yet. Despite my not understanding the plan, God's plan was being put into motion. The medical staff knew there would be nearly insurmountable challenges being deprived of oxygen for so long. I was numb to what the future could hold, but I could only focus on one thing for that moment. I prayed that Jim would survive. Let go and let God.

After an eternity, I was finally allowed to go to his room. Nothing could have prepared me for what I saw. Many large whirring machines, tubes, IVs, monitors, and staff existed. Their demeanor was somber, and I could see why they only gave Jim a 5 percent chance of surviving. I remember thinking will this be my final goodbye to Jim. Countless times in the past, when Jim would go to the hospital—they would stabilize him. Then I would be allowed into his room and be met by his contagious smile. This time I was met by a lifeless body that one could hardly see from all the equipment. I was only allowed to stay two minutes and then taken to a small private waiting room nearby.

Soon afterward. Jim's son Bryon and his friend joined me in this room. Jim's condition was critical and needed several different staff throughout the night. The medical team had asked us to remain close in this waiting room. It consisted only of a loveseat and one chair. The three of us sat in total silence and struggled to get through each minute that passed. When a staff member entered the room, we immediately went numb with uncontrollable fear. We dreaded the possibility of the news they may be bringing us. The dark hours of the night seemed endless, but we had no idea of the endless dark hours in the days ahead. Eventually, the morning light came, but the dark cloud remained.

LOOK FOR THE RAINBOW

Genesis 9:17 tells us—"So God said to Noah, "This [rainbow] is the sign of the covenant I have established between me and all life on the earth." Just as God paints His rainbow signature as a confirmation that He will ALWAYS be there for us, he also does not forsake us in times of trouble. We will not always face a world of rainbows, but God walks beside us when we struggle to see good. As I mentioned earlier, the verse from Psalm 32:7 speaks to this very moment in time. "You are my hiding place; You will protect me from trouble and surround me with songs of deliverance." This verse emphasizes that He will not keep us from trouble but protect us while we face trouble. Never lose faith or hope because He will be there every step of the way. The key to this verse is our acceptance of the results. I was angry at God for letting my mother pass away when I had just prayed for no more to handle. But we don't get to determine the outcome. Looking back, I don't know that my mother wouldn't have suffered many more years. There could have been more heart attacks, cancer, or possibly another stroke. This would have brought so much pain and suffering to her and

my dad. I needed to trust that God knew what was best, and we must accept that fact. Our only job is to rely on Him for comfort and healing when things don't go our way. I remember thinking this may be one of those times. I had to be strong and never stop looking for the rainbow.

Jim, along with divine intervention, had managed to survive the night. But now he was in an induced coma from lowering his body temperature. It was now March 18, 2010, and when I was allowed to enter his room again, I could see the full impact of his condition. They had added additional IVs overnight, and he was now up to twelve. The machine cooling his body made a haunting noise I will never forget. The large team of doctors was amazed that he had survived the night but made it very clear they had *not* increased his survival chance. It still loomed at only 5 percent. Now there was a new reality that the medical team was facing. Their previous reality was if Jim would even survive. Now they faced a second reality: if somehow, he *would* survive—just how much damage did he suffer from the cardiac arrest and lengthy lack of oxygen?

But we couldn't dwell on that now, as their immediate focus was keeping him alive. This was day one of a journey I was not prepared for. But it was a blessing that I could not see the road ahead. The fear I was facing nearly took my breath away, and that was without knowing the future. At the time, I was unsure where the deep-down strength came from to face the challenges ahead. But I knew I had to be strong for Jim, and hiding my fear was my only option. I kept my fear between God and myself.

As I mentioned, phase one was cooling Jim's internal body temperature to halt further organ damage. Phase two began later that evening and took place over the next few days. It was a slow process of raising his body temperature back up, but one that couldn't be rushed. Over the next week, Jim faced so many challenges. A fever spiked due to an unknown infection. He had suffered a collapsed lung, and several attempts at removing his ventilator were unsuccessful. Jim's blood pressure was all over the board. On March 19, it was 67/38 and was solely machine-driven as his heart was incapable on its own. His IVs increased again, and he now had thirteen. Each one had a massive job to do. Then, his blood pressure went sky-high in the following days, and his blood work showed multiple life-threatening problems. It was a full-time job for the doctors to find the right meds and doses and constantly monitor them. Things were changing almost by the minute, and with Jim barely alive, he had no extra strength to fight these problems.

There were minimal and brief signs of hope in the days ahead. The first came on March 21, five days after his cardiac arrest. The nurse came running to the cubicle where I had taken up residency. She grabbed me and said two words, "He's awake!" We both ran back to his room, and tears fell down my face. Since that first night, I had asked Jim many times to squeeze my hand. In this brief moment, he finally squeezed my hand, and I will never forget the feeling of thankfulness for the miracle God had just given me. It was the rainbow I had been watching for with all my might.

Sadly, the moment only lasted a few seconds, and he was again in a deep sleep. I was given another gift from God later that same day. I was lucky enough to be sitting at his bedside when it happened. They had stringent limits on how much I could be in his room due to his condition, all the equipment, and the large presence of medical staff. As I was sitting watching him, he very briefly opened his eyes and gave me a wink. A few seconds later, his eyes closed, and he returned to his deep sleep. But this miracle gave me the strength to keep going and not give up hope. It was my second rainbow of the day, and I could feel God's presence. But I'll be honest; this was a trying time for my faith. But deep down, I knew I couldn't give up and especially not give up for Jim's sake. He needed me and everyone in his corner who were praying and cheering him on this journey. Jim was so gravely ill and unaware of his army of believers. But that didn't stop the army. They kept marching forward with their prayers and support.

Further complications included a blood clot in his heart which had to be closely monitored. He had considerable fluid in his lungs, which complicated everything. He developed a cough, and the respirator tube made him very anxious, despite being semi-conscious. This went on to cause his blood pressure to rise to dangerous levels. In addition, they continued attempting to remove his breathing tube as it had been too long. Removing it would be a considerable risk but leaving it for this long was even riskier. His cough persisted, and his anxiety was very high. He received sedation to prevent further stress on his already se- verely damaged heart. Over time, this proved to be very chal- lenging.

They needed him to cough to help with the fluid build-up in his lungs. But they also needed him to remain calm and help resist his persistent urge to pull out the respirator tube. Finally, eleven days after his admittance and out of necessity, they were forced to remove the respirator tube, and thankfully it was suc- cessful. Until now, Jim could not speak because of the tube. No one knew the extent of his brain damage, but when the doctor asked him his name, he replied, "Jim." Hearing him speak was such a positive sign and music to my ears. He would face many serious hurdles neurologically over the following weeks. But for right now, at this very moment—we took the win. The doctor also asked Jim to smile, something no one could get him to do before now except for me. When asked, he turned his head towards me and gave me a smile I remembered and loved. But given the constant doctors hovering over his bed for the past eleven days and taking unbelievable amounts of blood for testing, putting tubes down his throat, inserting tubes into his veins, inserting balloon pumps, the constant changing out of IVs—I understood why he wasn't in the mood for smiling at them.

ONE STEP FORWARD— TWO STEPS BACK

New challenges were now presenting themselves, and one of the most alarming was he began to spike a fever. His white count was rapidly rising, and there was an infection lurking somewhere. He did not have the strength to take on another fight, so they ran blood gases to try and get more answers. He was given a special breathing mask, much to his disliking. This was to help push air in and ease his difficulty in breathing.

Anyone who knew Jim they were very aware of his sense of humor and, many would say, his stubbornness. We were getting glimpses of this soon after his respirator was removed. When his son, Bryon, said goodnight to him, Jim responded, "Byron—go get my dog!" His speech was slow—but we thanked God that he could speak. The next day when one of his nurses asked him to open his eyes, he shook his head no and smiled. Then he turned his head to look at me and winked. There was my Jim, and he was ever so slowly returning to us.

After the removal of the respirator, other issues presented themselves. Besides his fever which stayed between 101 and 102, they needed to get him out of bed. He didn't have the strength for this, and they used a lift to move him to the chair. Over the last twelve days, Jim had lost over thirty pounds and so much muscle mass. He needed pillows propped up around him to keep him in place.

Another problem that presented itself was a relentless case of hiccups. No one was sure why, but they could not get them stopped. Along with his cough, his fever, his weakness, and multiple IVs—hiccups were annoying. On March 29, Jim was again lifted into the chair, where he fell asleep. They let him remain asleep because he was still fighting the hiccups. Unfortunately, the hiccups lasted nearly sixty hours, and everyone said a prayer of thanks when they eventually stopped.

Jim's winks, smiles, and hand squeezing motivated me during this journey. I cannot even begin to imagine what was going through Jim's mind through all of this. The medical team said he did not remember what happened, and I am sure he was terrified. His sons were a huge motivation for him to keep fighting. Byron, who was at his side from the first night, along with Jeremy and Leo, who came to visit on March 24 and 25, inspired Jim not to give up. He was able to squeeze their hands as well, and I am sure it meant as much to them as it did to Jim. I will always be eternally grateful for their love and support, not only to Jim but also to me. It was a dark time for us all, and we each needed one another so very much.

My inspiration came from the endless prayers and support from Caring Bridge. I began a journal for Jim on March 18, one day after his cardiac arrest. The outpouring of kindness was overwhelming. To give you an indication of the number of people who repeatably wrote in his journal, here is a snapshot. I recently had Jim's entire Caring Bridge postings printed into a book. When I received the book, I was shocked that it totaled six hundred and seventy pages! It was a daily journal I wrote to help communicate his progress. But more importantly, it contained heartwarming messages from our friends and family. The book is such a treasure, and I sometimes use my journal entries as a reference for this book. I remember so clearly that March night back in 2010. But being able to read everyone's unending prayers and support for us was such a blessing. As Jim got stronger, I would read the comments from our friends and family, which brought tears to his eyes and mine.

Jim had several procedures done over the next few days, including a new balloon pump to assist his heart. His fever had dropped somewhat but was still persistent. His sodium level had risen, which needed to be monitored closely to prevent additional problems. On March 30, he was now down to only seven IVs, and when his nurse came into his room, he "informed" her that he was going home tomorrow. I had been reading Jim's comments from our dear neighbor Bill who had been caring for our dog, Gunner. Jim told the nurse he needed to get home to help his buddy, Bill, and see Gunner.

Through all this health scare, there was a positive side for our dog, Gunner. He was missing Jim terribly, and as I said, our dear neighbors Bill and Karen were helping with Gunner. Bill and his beloved dog would get in their wheeler and go down the gravel road to our home. There they would let Gunner out to run free around the farm. He was also feeding Gunner daily, which was such an act of kindness. It gave us one less thing to worry about when I had more than I could handle. But for Gunner— one day, he thought he had won the lottery. Another dear set of friends, Amber and Eric, drove over and shoveled some snow and thought they would help and feed our poor little starving Gunner. They did not know that Bill had fed him hours earlier. So, did Gunner say anything? Oh no…he kept quiet and gobbled up another bowl of dog food. At this point, I'm sure Gunner was hoping we had a third or possibly a fourth great set of friends to come over and help as well!

DON'T TAKE THE POPSICLE
FOR GRANTED

Later this day, a speech therapist asked Him to say "Ahh," which he did. Then she asked him to say "Ahh" again. He, with a mischievous smile, replied, "Ahh Again"! She then fed him some applesauce because he still could not have solid food. This was his first real food since he arrived at the hospital. He asked her for a cup of hot coffee, which she denied. After she left the room, he told me to get him some hot food! I needed to keep on the good side of the medical staff, so I reluctantly said, "Sorry."

A kidney specialist was added to his medical staff today and began treating some issues. His neurologist, cardiologist, and infectious disease doctors continued to monitor closely, especially his fever. Physical and speech therapists visited him daily to help with his muscle tone and coordination. Jim was taking baby steps in the right direction, and I was so thankful for each and every one.

On March 31, Jim's sense of humor appeared once again. First, he had finally beaten the hiccups and was sitting in his chair when a nurse came in to feed him some oatmeal. He was not yet able to hold a spoon, not to mention raise it to his mouth. As she was feeding him, she spilled oatmeal on his hospital gown. He looked at her mischievously and said, "You can't blame me for that one—you're *feeding me!"*

Later that day, we had a humbling moment. Things we take for granted every day were huge victories for Jim. He could hold a banana popsicle by himself today and eat it without assistance. That may not sound like much to some, but it was a huge deal for someone who had overcome so many odds and surprised all the Abbott Heart Hospital staff. We take so much of this life for granted. We can get up easily out of the chair and walk outside. We can feed ourselves without poking out our eyes with the spoon. We can go into the kitchen and get whatever food we want whenever we want. But for Jim, eating this popsicle was a huge deal, and he did NOT take it for granted. He didn't have to have anyone help him, and this simple task was a huge source of pride. Imagine being that happy to simply eat a popsicle on your own. The lesson here is don't take anything for granted! His hand and eye coordination showed minor signs of improvement every day, and these victories were humbly celebrated.

As one of his doctors said, "In all my career, I have never had a patient so close to death and facing that many critical health issues all at once!" He repeatedly said it was a miracle that Jim was still with us. He informed us that one of Jim's doctors, flown in during the first twenty-four hours, was one of the best in the world. He told the team he had never seen a patient so ill and so close to death yet survive. Glory be to God! Jim's will to survive and God's divine intervention kept him alive and were miracles before our eyes every day. Jim had an entire prayer warrior army, and God was answering. Here is where faith was so critical. I wanted answers on my timeline, and I had to trust God to allow Him to do things on His timeline. Little miracles presented themselves daily at this point in his journey; the only explanation was they were sent from above. Once again, *Let Go and Let God* and enjoy the popsicle.

SUPERMAN AND THREE HARD-BOILED EGGS

I believe with all my heart that God sends us earthly angels. An example of this for Jim was Amanda. During the first weeks of his care, I would sit in dark silence in the corner cubicle in the ICU waiting room. I had taken up residency and didn't leave the hospital. So many of those hours were shared with me by Amanda. She first met Jim when they worked together in the maintenance department at Cabela's. He became her mentor and taught her how to fix anything in the building. But along the way, he also taught her so much more. He instilled some traits that I'm sure are with her yet today. They had a very close bond, that was for sure.

He showed her the importance of working hard and never cutting corners in either work or life. He taught her the value of her work and to be proud of a job well done, no matter how small. He instilled the importance of always being prepared. This probably went back to his days as a troop leader for the Boy Scouts. Anyone who knew Jim knew his jeans pockets were like a walking hardware store. His pockets held as many nuts, bolts, screws, and nails as possible. When he'd empty his pockets before going to bed at night—the nightstand looked like aisle three at Hardware Hank. Looking back, Jim gave Amanda tools to fix a broken aquarium pump, but also essential tools for her life ahead. And now, in Jim's darkest hours, she was there for him. She was returning her support to the man who had given his support to a stranger just a few years earlier.

One of God's blessings happened on the very next day. On April 1, Jim was allowed to move from ICU to a regular room on the cardiac floor. We understood this did not mean he was out of the woods, but we were grateful for the development. Only one day later, on April 2, Jim faced a setback. He was unable to stand and was retaining dangerous levels of fluid. His kidneys had significantly suffered through the past sixteen days, and he now faced new hurdles. His hemoglobin had dropped dangerously low, and he was facing a transfusion.

In addition, he was also experiencing new neurological setbacks, which were difficult to manage. His body had gone through unbelievable trauma, and he was also taking an unbelievable number of medications. Together these two components began to cause Jim to hallucinate. The medical staff were confident that these would pass. They believed they could be a part of the healing process and encouraged me to go along with whatever he was experiencing. So, I would hear Jim sternly tell me to duck down for the next two days. He said a flock of geese was coming in, and I needed to duck so he could shoot them with his shotgun. So, I ducked—over and over. If anyone had walked by and seen me huddled in the corner, I probably would have also been admitted to the hospital. It might have been a different ward, though! Also, he would frequently tell me that he needed to fix the closet door. He said, "I don't know who built this place, but I need to reinforce that door!" At this point, he couldn't get out of bed, so I would tell him that once he was stronger, he could fix the closet door. But in his mind, he relived some memories he enjoyed—hunting and fixing anything broken. So, for two days, the theme was shotguns and screwdrivers. But I had to focus on being thankful to the Lord who had allowed him to remain alive. Not knowing what lay ahead, I had to be grateful for the moment.

On April 4, we celebrated Easter in his room together. His hemoglobin had dropped even more overnight, and he was given a blood transfusion to help offset the drop. This would hopefully help with his heart function as well as his energy. Later that day, he had some more milestones, including sitting on the edge of the bed unassisted. Physical therapy helped him into a chair, and he could pull himself up and stand for a few seconds. He did this not only once but three times! The therapist was amazed at this progress from just two days earlier. I called it our Easter miracle, and we had no words worthy enough to thank God.

I returned to work again at Cabela's on Monday, April 5. I would begin a new schedule of getting up at 4:00 a.m., working until 4:00 p.m., and then driving to Abbott until later in the evening. They had taken Jim to a procedure earlier this day to stop the drainage from a previous tube site. Over the past day, he had again taken a neurological hit and could not feed himself. Later that evening, his nurse came in to get his breakfast order. In a slow speech, he told her he wanted three hard-boiled eggs. She said she was sorry but that he could only have two. His facial expression showed his disagreement with her decision, and fast forward to Tuesday morning—there were three eggs on his breakfast plate. At this point, everyone had come to love Jim for his kindness and relentless determination. They were so inspired by all he had been through, and it became tough for the staff to say no to him. And he knew it!

This is where on his journey Jim was given the name Superman. People wrote of this in their Caring Bridge comments, and the medical staff would walk into his room and say, "How's it going, Superman?" This name was validated on April 7. Just five days earlier, Jim had gone through an evaluation to see if he was a candidate for Sister Kenny's Rehabilitation. They all agreed that he did not meet their qualifications and would be better served spending the rest of his life in a nursing home. We had faced earlier disappointments as well. They agreed to set up a heart transplant consultation in February because of Jim's frequent heart visits to Abbott over the past year. This process had begun only weeks before Jim's cardiac arrest. But now they had determined he did not have the "quality of life" necessary to be a transplant candidate. Therefore, he had been removed from the consultation, and all hope of possibly receiving a new heart was gone.

But here is where Superman showed his determination. Because of the progress Jim had shown over the past four days, the staff contacted Sister Kenny again and asked if they would be willing to do a second evaluation. They were skeptical, but four of their staff members came to his room and put him through a thorough series of tests. They all came to the same conclusion that he had made almost unbelievable progress since late last week. They went on to say they would gladly accept him into their program. So many prayers were once again answered. Just last week, it appeared that Jim's future only consisted of spending the rest of his life in a nursing home. But on this day, we were given hope that someday he could return to our home. Jim missed our country home and Gunner so much and it gave him the hope to continue fighting. Remember, we are never defeated unless we give up on God. Deuteronomy 31:8 reads, "The Lord himself goes before you and will be with you; He will never leave nor forsake you. Do not be afraid; do not be discouraged."

That evening after his evaluation, Superman once again showed his determination. He stood up out of his chair, grabbed his walker, and started walking to the doorway. He went out into the hall, and the nurses came scrambling to grab his IV stand and catch up. He miraculously made it almost to the end of the hall, where the nurses gave him a wheelchair escort back to his room. His endurance was gone when he returned, and they settled him back into bed. The nurses talked with him about how he likes to give them some "friendly" grief. They all agreed that they enjoyed it, which made for a fun shift at work. He replied, "Well, at least now I can remember each of you. It makes it easier to know who I have teased now!" From then on, the nursing staff would request to be assigned to Jim; he loved every minute! When the nurse enters his room at night for his breakfast order, they automatically say, "Three hard-boiled eggs, right?" Superman had not lost his faith and wouldn't go down without a fight.

IF YOU'RE GOING TO WORRY...DON'T BOTHER TO PRAY

Over the next few days, some of his IVs were removed, and some were added as blood work showed concerns. He was on many pills, and when the staff would come in to administer his meds, they would always ask him his name and birthday. After a few days of this, the next time a nurse came in and asked him for this info, he replied, "You keep asking for my name and birthday—you must be having memory issues!" The staff were so used to this now that they would take his temperature if he didn't tease them.

Jim was preparing to make the transition to Sister Kenny. It was adjacent to Abbott, so the move was convenient. He needed to be off all IVs for twenty-four hours before they allowed the move. They agreed to have him leave Abbott on Mon, April 12—twenty-six days after his admittance. Jim's cardiac doctors spent hours every day with Jim over the past month, and once again, prayers were answered. On April 13, the next day after moving to Sister Kenny, I received a telephone call from the cardiac transplant team. They agreed to reschedule his transplant consultation because of Jim's incredible progress over the past twelve days. I almost fell to my knees hearing this news and couldn't wait to share it with Jim. I knew it didn't mean a transplant was a definite go, but it did mean we had hope once again. As you can imagine, the outpouring of prayers and support on Caring Bridge from this news was astounding and again brought tears to Jim's eyes. The transplant team decided to hold the consultation on May 17 to give him time for rehabilitation.

Each day on this journey had been a gift; now, we had even more hope for the future. Not only the possibility of Jim returning home from rehab but also given another chance at possibly receiving the gift of a heart transplant. As I knew it would happen, once Jim began his residency at Sister Kenny, it would only be a matter of time before he began his initiation of the staff. On day two, when they entered his room for meds and asked him his name and birthday—he calmly replied, "I don't know." They got a look of panic until they saw his smirky smile.

A few weeks earlier, in ICU, one of Jim's machines and my foot had a battle, and sadly the machine won. It had been sore ever since. But being preoccupied with Jim and his care, I ignored the fact that it was swollen and painful every night. The staff finally talked me into going to the ER at Abbott and getting X-rays. Thankfully, it was not broken, but it had a severe tissue injury. It was no big deal, but at least now I knew what was wrong. The staff had come to love us, and we were now known at Sister Kenny as Superman and Lois Limpy Lane.

There is one trait in humanity that is ever-present. It has seemed to multiply as our world becomes so much faster-paced. This trait is our lack of patience. We want things now. We go through the drive-thru because it's fast. We become impatient if the line is long. We switch the channels repeatedly, searching for something that interests us. We throw a frozen meal into the microwave because it's quick. We drive five to seven miles per hour over the speed limit. Just saying…I may or may not be guilty of this! We take the freeway as opposed to the scenic route. We order from Amazon to get the package only hours later. And God help us if our purchase doesn't arrive until the following day. The list goes on and on and on.

We have become such an impatient society, and we go through our day missing such obvious gifts from God that he puts in our path. Choose to exit the main highway and make time to find the beauty of a rolling pasture filled with wildflowers and horses along the scenic route. Take time to not opt for the drive-thru but go inside and possibly brighten the day of a worker who needs our smile to keep going. Take time to put down the remote and go for a leisurely walk in the woods and possibly catch a glimpse of a doe and her fawn in the shadows.

I wasn't any different than this in the early days of Jim's cardiac arrest. I prayed to God but wanted my results in my time. I wanted Jim to wake up, for the fever to leave, for him to be able to walk, to speak—all things I thought should happen in my timeline. But God is the one in control. We can try and go through this thing called life by ourselves. Another option is to take God's hand and let him lead us through it all - the good as well as the bad. We still need to pray earnestly, but also, we need to accept the outcome, whatever it may be.

A challenge for me in my daily life is one of the most difficult I face. This challenge would be to NOT worry after praying. We pray to God for something we want and then turn around and worry about it throughout the day. It is easy to do this because worry is a human trait we have trouble shaking. When we pray… then turn around and worry about what we just prayed for… it is counterproductive. It is like we are saying, "God, I prayed but am not sure if You can handle it." If we are going to worry, don't bother praying because, in my mind, worry cancels the prayers. So, pray, have faith, let go and let God handle whatever it is. You will have peace and much less stress, and who doesn't want that? The bottom line is you only get one or the other—prayer or worry. The two don't mix and never will.

So, our job is to keep praying; when God sends an answer, we must accept it. This is especially true when it wasn't what we had hoped for. We think we know what is best for our lives but cannot see the future. We must walk with God trusting Him completely until we are called home.

Here are some bible verses that I lean on daily, and my hope and prayer is that they may also help you. Philippians 4:6-7 reads, "Do not be anxious about anything, but in everything by prayer and petition, with thanksgiving present your requests to God. And the peace of God, which transcends all understanding, will guard your hearts and minds in Christ Jesus." Philippians 4:13, "I can do everything through Him who gives me strength." I Peter 5:7 says, "Cast all your anxiety on Him because He cares for you." Matthew 6:25-29 explains the concept of worry so well. "Therefore, I tell you, do not worry about your life, what you will eat or drink, or your body, what you will wear. Is life not more important than food, and the body more important than clothes? Look at the birds of the air; they neither sow nor reap or store away in barns, yet your heavenly Father feeds them. Are you not much more valuable than they? Who of you can add a single hour to his life by worrying? And why do you worry about clothes? See how the lilies of the field grow. They do not labor or spin. Yet I tell you that not even Solomon in all his splendor was dressed like one of these." Finally, Matthew 6:34 sums it up for us, "Therefore do not worry about tomorrow, for tomorrow will worry about itself. Each day has enough trouble of its own."

THANKFUL FOR BRIEF WINS

R eturning to Jim's journey, on April 17, five days after his move to Sister Kenny, I was permitted to take Jim in his wheelchair back across the street to Abbott's fourth-floor ICU. They called ahead to let them know we were on our way. When we exited the elevator, the staff came running to see Superman. They were amazed at his progress in the past five days; it was a great reunion and personal therapy for Jim. Another form of healing therapy for Jim was listening to me read his Caring Bridge comments. Through everything that had happened so far, we both had so many blessings to be thankful for, and we never lost sight of that. God was at work in our lives every day, and we both sincerely hoped that our inspiration would be seen by everyone who viewed his Caring Bridge page. We hoped that we could give others hope for their lives for whatever they were facing. No one is meant to walk this life alone.

Jim went through hours every day of physical and occupational therapy. Despite initially thinking he would be there for at least a month—he was given the green light to go home on April 22, only eleven days after being admitted. This was a big win for Jim, and he gratefully accepted it. But now, looking back, it was a gift from God that we could not see what lay ahead from this win. It would prove to be a brief win, but at the end of the day, it was still a win. The reunion with Jim and Gunner was emotional. We were so blessed with caring neighbors and friends who helped care for Gunner for the past thirty-six days. But seeing Jim and Gunner back together was a sight I'll never forget. It was as if invisible Velcro was keeping them attached at the hip. Not sure who needed who more.

The following week was filled with physical therapy, resting, and enjoying the deck with Gunner. Jim was so happy to be home; his unbelievable progress blessed us. But Jim's stay at home was about to be threatened. It had been another brief win on his journey, but now the win was fading. On April 30, eight days after returning home from Sister Kenny, I had to call the ambulance as Jim had difficulty breathing. They took him to Monticello, where they quickly transferred him to Abbott. An hour later, the transplant team arrived in his room and said, "Superman, we knew you'd be back—we just didn't expect it this soon!"

Over the next week, the plans were to perform open heart surgery by installing a pump. But this was halted when tests revealed a small mass in the lungs. This needed to be identified with a biopsy to eliminate cancer. This would have ended all surgery discussions. It was found to be a rare fungus known to the SW United States. It was determined he likely developed this while doing road construction in Arizona. The desert dust had more than likely been the cause. But because it was treatable and given the severity of his existing heart, the decision was made to immediately move up his transplant consult, which was still nearly a week and a half away. The medical team all agreed that the clock was ticking for Superman. His heart was rapidly deteriorating, and the decision was made to put him on the transplant waiting list immediately. Because he struggled so much with fluid around his heart and his kidney functions were severely compromised—the decision was made that Jim should not return home as the risks were too great. Instead, his new temporary address would be the fourth floor of Abbott Heart Hospital. It was now May 9, and day fifty-four on his journey. Despite this decision, Jim was thankful for his brief win of leaving Sister Kenny and going home. He was just as thankful for spending eight days at home before it became necessary to return to Abbott. Jim never once complained about the length of these wins, but he focused on being blessed to have been given the wins in the first place. But now, we needed to focus on what lies ahead on his ever-challenging journey.

GOD WHISPERED

This chapter is where the title of my book will begin to show its presence. Ordinarily, Jim's fear of the unknown would be almost more than we could handle. He had overcome unbelievable odds, but we had to be realistic. How many more chances could one get? His nickname Superman had held up through it all so far, but the odds kept circling back, and they weren't in his favor. But I know now, by the grace of God, I felt a calm and a huge presence of peace come over me. It was an intense feeling I had not felt up to this time. It is so hard to describe, but I knew I wasn't alone in that moment. God was at my side, and it was as if I could hear Him speak, "I've got this." A feeling of peace was present that I could not explain at a time when I should have only felt fear. It would ultimately be understandable at this moment not to experience peace. But I had peace when it made *no sense* to have peace. We were both facing an uncertain future, knowing that at any moment, Jim's heart could stop beating, and his heroic journey would be over instantly. But Jim's prayer warriors were not giving up, and we couldn't either. So, the faint voice would become our guiding light in whatever lies ahead. God whispered to us both, "I've got this."

After this moment, I felt relieved that Jim was remaining at Abbott. I knew he would have constant supervision, which I couldn't provide when working. Plus, the ambulance was getting so used to coming to our home I think they programmed our address into their GPS. It had reached the point when they arrived at our home and walked inside, the first words out of their mouth were, "Hello, Gunner." This doctor's decision removed the stress of having Jim home alone, and I felt a relief I hadn't had before. I knew he would be in good hands and have the best chance to handle whatever lies ahead.

Three days later was a big one for Jim! We got approval to bring Gunner to visit him on the fourth floor. The staff, who had heard so much about Jim's wonder dog, fell in love at first sight. They would find any excuse to come into his room so that they could pet Gunner. Even Jim's doctor would make extra daily visits whenever Gunner came to visit. But Gunner was not a fan of the elevator. But once the doors opened, he knew exactly where Jim's room was, and I had all I could do to keep him from getting away and running down the hall. Once he got to his room, he jumped up on the bed and would never leave Jim's side. The staff at first wasn't so sure about this. But just as with the three hard-boiled eggs, they found it hard to say no. When they saw how much it meant to Jim—they realized he needed this therapy more than anything else, even if it meant a few dog hairs.

The following few days became very challenging for Jim. He faced nausea and vomiting, along with elevated liver enzyme levels. He began quickly losing weight again and became very weak. His heart was pumping at a very low level, and this caused a massive amount of fluids around his lungs and heart. To help alleviate this, he would be administered medication to offset the fluid. But there was a downside to this plan. The meds were extremely hard on his kidneys and they were approaching failure. Consequently, when the fluid meds were again lowered to prevent kidney failure, the fluid around the heart would gain momentum. The medical staff had to walk a fine line to keep both in check.

A dear friend of ours, Vicki, employed at the heart hospital, was kind and brought Jim a card table and a dog puzzle for his room. She was a fantastic source of support for me in the early days and for us as Jim continued his journey. She was most definitely an angel sent from God to help us through this difficult and frightening time. In addition, to help Jim pass the time, the nursing staff brought him a toy gun that shot foam darts, along with a target and a foam basketball and hoop. I was sure that would make things interesting when Gunner was to return in a few days. Everyone was kind to help Jim pass the endless hours with puzzles and toys. Before this, Jim watched the cooking channel all day because he had nothing else to do. I am guessing he alone raised their TV ratings off the chart. The nurses would ask him if he had any new recipes to share. Jim had always been a good cook, but now he was enhancing his skills.

One thing that was on Jim's mind and was bothering him was his garden. In the past years, he had planted many tomatoes, peppers, onions, cilantro—all the fixings for homemade salsa. He and Amanda had canned huge numbers of quarts and pints and he could only think that it may not happen this year. So, on my day off, I first went to Abbott and left for home early. I tilled the garden, which was huge, by the way, and got his tomato plants in the ground right before dark. He was so relieved and thankful when I told him the next day. Jim's determination was so inspiring. He never doubted that he would return home to make salsa —his only worry was getting the garden tilled and planted. God worked through me for Jim's garden, whispering, "I've got this."

WE'RE SO SORRY

On May 25, the transplant team decided to perform another right heart cath to reevaluate the performance of his heart. But through it all, Superman kept his sense of humor. They were doing blood pressure checks every fifteen minutes, and when the nurse came in to do his next reading, he said, "What should I do —I can't breathe." The nurse got a panicked look, and then there it was…his smirky smile. She told him she would straighten his curls if he didn't behave. For those of you who knew Jim, his long hair and curls were to be touched by no one. When she returned fifteen minutes later, he asked if she would also check his oxygen level. She answered, "I'd better. You are so full of wind. Who knows what it will read!"

The following day, May 26, the team immediately moved Jim back into ICU. He had changed rooms all around the fourth floor of the heart hospital and now, once again, was moving. He was facing multiple health problems. His heart was failing, and his kidneys and liver were facing challenges. He was not feeling well and was becoming very weak. Because of this turn of events, the medical team decided to move Jim up on the transplant waiting list. The team knew his time was limited, and the clock was ticking. His heart was failing, and a donor needed to be found soon. So, Jim moved to the ICU unit, where his damaged heart would hopefully keep beating until a match could be found.

The days ahead brought a new challenge neither of us had faced. The criteria to find a donor match is unbelievably complicated. Shortcuts cannot be made for obvious reasons, and a detailed cross-evaluation is performed. The team lets you know when they have a possible donor, and for the next few hours, you wait while the final tests are performed. We got this notice on May 28, only two days after his move to ICU. We were waiting for the final word on a donor and a new lease on life. But after a few hours, the doctor entered Jim's room and said, *"We're so sorry."* We were informed that the heart was not a complete match and would not happen. Something they saw at the last minute prevented them from going ahead with the transplant.

This was where we needed to hold on to those three words, "I've got this." We weren't prepared for the roller coaster ride; the letdown was devastating. But we kept our faith, knowing that all of this was in God's hands. We understood that Jim's time was running out, but praying and then worrying, as I said earlier, was not an option. So, we prayed and then turned it over to God. He had brought us this far, but we knew only God held the future. We just had to keep the faith…no matter what. It is hard to describe the emotions I was facing and was sure Jim was facing. No one knew if Jim's heart would continue to beat until a donor could be found. This was a test like none other in cherishing our moments on this earth with our loved ones. This test certainly wasn't just isolated to Jim. Every person walking this life on earth has absolutely no guarantee about what the next minute, hour, day, month, or year will bring. So, my message to everyone reading this is to please cherish every moment God gives you. Every day count your blessings and hug your loved ones.

On May 30, we were informed again that there may be a possible match. We did our best not to get our hopes up. We had to believe it would happen if it were to be. This time it was proven to be a perfect match. But given the fact that the donor was in Dallas, Texas, and the distance needed to transport the heart successfully, made this impossible. So once again, the doctor came into Jim's room and said those three words, *"We're so sorry."* Again, a roller coaster ride that I wouldn't wish on anyone. This time was again a test of our faith. And once again, I'll be honest—it would have been easier to give up. But by God's grace, we didn't give up and kept fighting Jim's struggle for survival.

In the days ahead, despite waiting on a donor and Jim's heart failing—he was able to share some extraordinary times with the staff. As I had mentioned earlier, Jim was an expert salsa maker and had canned many jars the previous two summers. The staff shared our desperation for a donor, and everyone watched his heart deteriorate. On June 3, the fantastic ICU staff agreed on the plan that was about to happen. From day one, the heart hospital senior staff coordinator and now close friend Vicki went above and beyond. She brought a vegetable chopper, a chopping block, and all the ingredients to make fresh salsa into Jim's room. The smile on his face was worth a million dollars. It took his mind off his health and the nausea he was still facing. Despite his weakening strength, he persevered, and they made a fresh batch of salsa together. He was so tired afterward but so pleased as well. This simple act of kindness gave him purpose when he needed it most. The salsa was refrigerated overnight until the next day. On June 4, Vicki returned, and the three of us had a picnic in Jim's room with chips and salsa. It was such a nice change of pace for him, especially after eighty days of hospital food.

To help lighten the mood of Jim's endless waiting for a heart—a dear family member, Mavis, put an entry on Caring Bridge that brought a smile to Jim's face. Mavis and her husband Dan had a dog named Jessie Lu, and the dog "typed" an entry on Jim's page saying—"Jim, please do not feed Gunner any salsa. My parents gave me enchilada sauce once, and let's say…it wasn't a pretty picture!" From humor—to support—to prayers…everyone was such a blessing to us with their loving comments on Caring Bridge. God had given us an army of followers to cheer us along, and we were so grateful.

Jim was a favorite on the floor, and everyone loved him. Just as on the other wing, the nurses would request to be assigned to him. They all said they had never had a patient so kind and appreciative of all they did for him. Even when they would come in to stick a needle in his arm for blood, he would always say thank you to them. I think the whole world could learn from Jim. If we all used those two words more often with one another —*thank you*—what a better place this would be. They were also so amazed that he never complained. Someone who had been through so much and had every right—he just never did. Another trait they loved about him was his sense of humor. Their days in ICU could get long and stressful, and he never disappointed by bringing a smile to their face with his teasing.

He could wrap them around his finger because he convinced them to let Gunner visit him in ICU. The staff from the other wing that had cared for him for so long heard that Gunner was in the house. They came over to see him again, and both Gunner and Jim loved every minute. They both were celebrities on the fourth floor, and Jim was so blessed to have such a caring and compassionate medical team helping to keep him alive.

Jim has been wearing Superman pajama bottoms exclusively in the hospital for some time now. When Jim would go downstairs for tests in the cath lab, the staff first looked for his Superman pants. If he happened not to be wearing them, they loved telling him to get with the program! Some of our friends and even a staff member brought him some extra Superman pants, so he never had to face the shame of going to the cath lab again without his legendary pajamas. On June 6, Jim moved to a larger room in ICU with a better view. This room had a recliner for me, which I greatly appreciated. I was able to go see Jim every day after work for about four hours. Gunner was not happy and wished he could visit again. Our dear neighbors, whom I mentioned earlier, were terrific. They cared for Gunner and made these long days and nights possible. We couldn't have gotten through all of this without them.

By now, Jim had received many presents of Superman merchandise. He was even given a Superman thong which was hung from his IV pole! Not sure who that was for or who it would fit —but it sure got a lot of second looks from the staff! The doctor even joked he would wear it over his medical coat if it meant Jim could find a donor! Jim had become quite the legend, and everyone was pulling for him to win this battle. He had touched the hearts of the staff, and it showed. They became our "family" and were another layer of strength for us both.

On June 11, we got word of another possible donor. This would be round three, and we again got our hopes up. Jim's health with each passing day was getting worse. His heart could not keep up and was functioning at only a fraction. The hospital got word the match was perfect, and we began to call the family with the fantastic news. Our roller coaster ride would not be repeated, and the hope in Jim's eyes shone. Then the doctor entered Jim's room and repeated those three words, *"We're so sorry."* The team on the other end had found a very small blockage in the donor's heart, which canceled the procedures. Once again, we had to remind ourselves that this was God's plan, and we needed to trust and let go. It hurt deeply, but we held on to those three words, "I've got this." It was now day eighty-seven.

The next few days brought many scares. Jim's heart was rapidly failing, and he had episodes of chest pain, dizziness, and bleeding from his heart cath. He still never lost his faith and never complained. He continued to thank each staff member as they cared for him. Without even realizing it, he brought a new awareness of gratitude to so many people by his actions. We think our life is ruined if we get into a fender bender, fall and break our leg, or get hurt by a friend. Here was a man hanging on for dear life and still thankful for every breath he could take.

On June 20, Father's Day, the nurse asked Jim what he wanted for the day. He replied, "A beer." She smiled and said she would be right back. She got some paper, drew a Coors label, and taped it to a can of Sprite. She returned and said to Jim, "This is as good as it's going to get!" He greatly appreciated the effort and enjoyed his Sprite—day ninety-six.

THE ULTIMATE SACRIFICE

O n June 24, day one hundred, we again got word a donor was found. After all the false alarms, we knew to be cautious. This donor's heart looked promising, and they took Jim off all food at 6:00 a.m. I had plans to bring Gunner to Abbott that day. But upon receiving a call from Jim a little later, he said I should probably leave Gunner at home just in case. I went to work and anxiously waited for news. As I said, we had been down this road before. We both asked ourselves, "Could this be it?" Then I got the call at work that this was the real deal. The transplant was a go, and I was instructed to head to the hospital immediately. I have no words for how I felt. I could only imagine what Jim was feeling. No more "We're so sorry"; believing this could be our moment was hard to imagine. I gathered my things at work like I had a caffeine IV drip! My strong support team of some of my managers and team members ran out to the car to see me off. I had made this trip to Abbott so many times before. The first one was back on March 17, not knowing if Jim was alive. Since then, there have been so many trips where the future was uncertain. And now I was taking another trip to

Abbott with the possibility of Jim getting the miracle we had all hoped for from the beginning. My emotions were bouncing around inside of me like a pinball machine.

At the hospital, we were told things could still change, but this time looked very promising. We kept our guarded optimism, knowing that God was in charge. In the early afternoon, Jim's favorite from the heart hospital (his salsa-making partner) called him. She said she had heard that a heart was possibly found and wanted to know if we knew anything more. While talking on the phone, she told Jim, "As long as you're just lying there waiting...could you help me with my lasagna recipe?" Again, the friendships Jim made and the endless days of watching the cooking channel while hospitalized were a blessing to be shared.

Here is where a divine miracle from God was performed —one of so many Jim had already experienced. But this one was different—it would change Jim's world. The donor family was preparing to say goodbye to their loved one. This is something I cannot even imagine—the act of removing life support from someone so close and dear to you. This all along has been a huge weight on both Jim and me. For him to survive, another life must be sacrificed. It is something that a recipient of an organ must face each and every day they are alive. They were given a second chance at life when someone else lost a life. It is heavy to handle.

But there was a problem. The transplant team at Abbott had just begun another heart transplant because a donor was located earlier the same day for that patient. One transplant in a day at Abbott was a big deal, but two transplants in the same day were unheard of and never happened. The timeline for a transplant is planned down to the minute. They needed to continue with the eight-hour transplant surgery that they had already begun. But this meant that Jim's donor family could not take their loved one off from life support at this time. For obvious reasons, the heart cannot be harvested until the last moment before it begins its' air travel to the recipient.

With the clock ticking and the window of opportunity fading, Jim's social worker and transplant coordinator contacted the donor family. They were informed of the situation and were presented with a proposition. It was made very clear that they would make this decision. It had to be theirs and theirs alone. They were asked if they would postpone their final goodbye by six hours and hold off on ending life support for their loved one. This would allow the transplant team to complete their current surgery and get Jim prepped for his transplant. They were told of the seriousness of Jim's health, and by the grace of God, they unselfishly agreed.

To this day, I am still amazed at this ultimate sacrifice they made at a time when their grief had to be overwhelming. This was another "I've got this" from God. Their decision brought tears to our eyes, as well as the staff at Abbott. It would have been so easy, and understandably so, to deny our request and not prolong their agony. But Jim was given a chance at surviving with their incredible gift and ultimate sacrifice.

Here is when things got wild. We had been forewarned that everything would happen almost instantly once a heart was found and matched. It was June 24 at 3:30 p.m., and ten staff came rushing into Jim's room. They told me I could stay but needed to stand in the corner to make room. They proceeded to take fourteen large vials of blood. Until now, we were accustomed to the usual tube for a blood draw. These tubes were like nothing we had seen before. I remember thinking they almost looked like lab beakers from my high school biology class days.

These things were huge, and I couldn't believe how much blood they held. Everyone was scurrying around, and the scene was quite chaotic. Jim just laid there and watched it all go down. Everyone knew exactly what their role was, and they executed it flawlessly. I was amazed at how calm Jim was, and I could feel his peace while I stood in awe in the corner.

Once they had completed what they came in to do, they informed us that he would be rushed down to surgery. Four staff members grabbed his IVs and bed and ran down the hall. I ran alongside him and said, "I love you." We didn't even have time to say what we were both thinking, but we knew by our glance that whatever happened from here on out was in God's hands. I stood by as they wheeled him into the elevator and watched the doors close. I remember standing there alone and wondering if he would survive and if I would ever see him alive again. His heart was so damaged from the cardiac arrest, and the risks and dangers of him even surviving the removal of his heart were so uncertain. And if he did survive that procedure, he would still be facing many hours of surgery to implant his new heart. With every ounce of my strength, I held on to God's whisper, "I've got this."

MORE WHAT-IF'S

Here is where everything gets so time-sensitive. The preparation for his transplant would take about three hours and include opening his entire chest wall. The doctors finished their first transplant and had a ten-minute break for a cup of coffee. The coordination that goes into an organ transplant is unbelievable. The donor's heart was now being prepared for harvest and the helicopter trip to Minneapolis.

The transplant doctors began their prep surgery at 4:00 p.m. They maintained constant contact with the medical team for the donor's heart to ensure nothing went wrong. Everything is planned right out to the minute. Once the helicopter transporting the donor's heart got closer to Abbott, this was communicated to the doctors, and they began prep to remove Jim's heart from his chest cavity. He would then be living only with the aid of a machine and ready for his new gift of life—the heart transplant on day one hundred.

After Jim had been taken down for surgery, I returned to my waiting room cubicle—my home away from home. My dear sister-in-law, Mavis, was with me, and I was so thankful I wasn't alone. She helped keep me calm in what was an almost unbearable wait. Nearly three hours later, we received an update that Jim's prep had gone successfully, and he was ready for phase two. So many prayers from us and Jim's prayer army were being spoken this night, and prayer's power was my strength.

But the endless hours of waiting did give way to worry. I fought with my inner self and began going through "what ifs." What if something goes wrong on the donor's end, and Jim's chance is lost? What if Jim doesn't survive this critical and lengthy surgery, and this journey would all be for nothing? What if the doctors who had already performed a transplant—kind of a big deal—were not on the top of their game for round two? This was Satan's work at his best. Put doubt in our minds and weaken our faith—it is what he loves the most. My mind raced, but I dug down deep, and God's three words, "I've got this," came back to the forefront. I held on to His whisper with my every breath and pushed the what-ifs out of my mind.

What happened next is something I will never forget and relive still today. On June 24, day one hundred, at 7:06 p.m., I heard and felt something almost supernatural. Sitting in my cubicle, I saw flashing lights in the night sky out of the corner of my eye. I heard an eerie whirring sound and then saw the sight I still play in my mind today. The whirring and the lights were from the helicopter that carried Jim's new heart. The landing pad for Abbott's airlift helicopters was only a few floors above where I sat. The first thing that flashed through my mind was that a family had unselfishly given this gift, landing just floors overhead. Their ultimate sacrifice, which had to be so painful, was about to save Jim's life, hopefully. It was almost too much to absorb, and I felt such a range of emotions. Thankfulness, empathy, and fear, but I clung to hope most of all.

We had one of the best medical teams in the country about to attempt to save Jim's life. The miracles from God kept coming, and this was the biggest of them all. And just so you know, they do transport the heart in a small cooler. I had visions of the personnel running from the helicopter with the precious cargo safely inside an Igloo cooler. This transport medical team was a small but incredibly essential part of the vast number of doctors and nurses who had gotten Jim to this point. Each was integral to the lengthy process, and we were very thankful for their unwavering dedication.

The following hours seemed endless. Sitting in my cubicle with Mavis, I couldn't even imagine the scene in surgery. A team had already performed an eight-hour surgery and was now at it again. The waiting for this nearly matched all the waiting over the past one hundred days combined.

At 12:45 a.m., June 25, the transplant team walked into my cubicle and gave us a thumbs up. Once again, God's word rang true, "I've got this!" It wasn't so much a whisper this time but a glorious shout! The doctors went on to explain that it was a complicated surgery. Jim's heart was even worse than all the tests indicated. They explained Jim's ejection fraction, the blood percentage pumped out of a filled ventricle with each heartbeat. According to the American Heart Association, an average ejection fraction ranges from 50 to 75 percent. A borderline fraction can range from 41 to 50 percent, indicating heart failure. Percentages below 40 can become a ticking time bomb. Jim's ejection fraction was 15 percent! Enough said.

I always knew we had made it this far by God's grace. But that night, it was more evident than ever before. So many prayers were answered, and God wasn't ready for Jim to leave this earth. We had to face reality and know he was not out of the woods. We held tightly to God's reassurance in Deuteronomy 31:6 "Be strong and courageous. Do not be afraid or terrified because of them, for the Lord your God goes with you; he will never leave or forsake you." But we were well aware we would need to draw on God's strength in the future and be thankful for what God had provided up to this point.

A NEW DAY ONE

June 25, 2010, was not day 101. We renamed it Jim's new day one. Jim was given a second chance at life; this was his new birthday, and we couldn't thank God enough. We did not know how many more days Jim would be allowed, but right now, we celebrated this day—day one. Jim was once again back in ICU and on a respirator. He had several IVs, along with three chest tubes draining blood. That morning a nurse came into his room and asked if he remembered that he was there to get a new heart. He nodded yes. She told him his new heart was beating, and his eyes got very big. They needed him to remain calm and wanted him to rest, so I returned to my cubicle "home."

A few hours later, they removed his ventilator, and he breathed independently. I walked into his room, and the first words out of his mouth were, "Hey, how's it going?" He reached for my hand and had tears rolling down his cheeks. Mavis and Jim's son, Jeremy, were there with us, and he spoke to each of them. He had considerable pain, which was to be expected. But he was fully alert and even asked to eat, even though solid foods were a no at this time. But you can't blame him for trying. But he did receive his first meal with his new heart—Cream of Wheat and yogurt. It was a start, and he was thankful.

Later that same day, they removed the tube from his leg, and he had to lay flat and still for two hours. Their plan also began to slowly, one by one, remove some of the IVs from his surgery. He was exhausted but was a happy camper when he got a banana popsicle for his evening meal. He had come a long way since the banana popsicle he first ate when recovering from cardiac arrest. These popsicles have always been a favorite of his—actually, anything banana. He loved banana bread, banana cream pie, and just bananas by themselves. So, this popsicle was a big treat for him after a tough day.

His evening nurse had never worked with Jim as she was new to the floor. I warned her of Jim's antics, and she said the staff had already clued her in. They were all jealous that she was assigned to Jim and not them. That evening something unexpected happened. If you remember back to day five, Jim developed a sixty-hour relentless case of hiccups. Well, they were back. They were trying different remedies, but so far, with no luck. When I was getting ready to leave his room for the night and go to my cubicle, I told him I would be there all night. He smiled and replied, "So will I!"

June 26, 2010—a new day two. Jim was assisted today out of bed and into a chair. He is on significant pain medication but has graduated to soft foods. Today he ate tomato soup and pudding for his noon and evening meals. Jim's hiccups had stopped for a while but had now returned. His chest was so sore from the top to bottom incision, so hiccups were not especially fun for him. In addition, the anti-rejection drugs necessary for his transplant were messing with his blood sugars. They ranged from seventy to three hundred and forty, but we were told that was to be expected. They had him on an insulin drip and were challenged because they kept having to turn it on and off again to regulate his sugars.

He needed to remain as close to a germ-free environment as possible for obvious reasons. The anti-rejection drugs lower your immune system so the body does not reject the new heart. He was in one of the beautiful fashion-minded hospital gowns he loved so much! He told me he needed his Superman pajamas and hoped he would get the ok to wear them soon. The whiteboard in his room under his name stated "Jim, aka Superman," so he had a legend to uphold.

June 28, 2010—a new day four. Jim continued his slow path of healing. Today he walked around the ICU unit, and they were able to lose another three IVs. He saw one of the nurses caring for him in the ICU unit before his transplant. She was standing in the hallway, and he told her to get busy and quit scouting out all the guys in their hospital gowns! She replied with a big smile, "Oh Jim, you just keep quiet and keep walking!" And this is why they loved him so much!

They planned to move him out of ICU today but felt it best to give it at least one more day. He was on an unbelievable number of meds and was nauseous because of them. His incisions were at risk every time he vomited, to say nothing of the pain, so this needed to get under control. This week we were told we will begin our education on the medications once he is discharged, along with the game plan for the next few months. There would be countless appointments with weekly biopsies to ensure there was no rejection of the heart.

June 30, 2010—new day six. Today Jim moved out of ICU and over to the other wing of the fourth floor. They had removed all his IVs and he was only on a portable heart monitor. He took all his meds in pill form, which was going well. Jim could go outside for the first time in months and get some fresh air. There is a balcony off the fourth floor waiting room, and we sat there for nearly an hour. Fresh air and sunshine are something we take for granted every day, but for Jim, this was such a blessing. He said he would never forget the feeling of the breeze and the warmth of the sunshine on his face.

Jim had his first biopsy today. They go through the artery into the new heart and take a tiny snip to test for rejection. These biopsies get scored with a 1R equaling a mild rejection. 2R equals moderate rejection, and 3R equals severe rejection. The goal score is zero indicating the body fully accepts its new resident—the transplanted heart. Later that afternoon, we got the news of Jim's score—a zero! This entire journey has been a miracle, and it continued today. No words could express thanks enough for Jim's prayer army on Caring Bridge for always being there and always having hope.

July 1, 2010—new day seven. An echocardiogram was performed on Jim today, and they found something that needed further investigation. They will put him under tomorrow and go in with a camera to examine the heart and determine the status. Their main concern is a blood clot which would be devastating. I knew my emotions would get the best of me, and I would start worrying. So, as I have said so many times before, I clung to the words, "I've got this." I repeated them over and over and hung on ever so tightly. I gave it to God, and that was my lifeline. Jim had come so far; beat the worst odds, and I knew that God's plan was what would happen in the end. It was a true test of faith, but I owed it to God, who had already given us so much.

July 2, 2010—new day eight. Jim went down for his test at 9:00 a.m. and returned to his room a little before noon. They determined that what they saw on the echo did not present any problems, and a blood clot was ruled out. We were both so thankful for not having to face another complication. We returned to the fourth-floor patio for some more fresh air and sunshine. Later that afternoon, the transplant team told us that Jim would go home tomorrow if everything continued well. Home! What a great-sounding word, especially since this journey began on March 17. The next day was Saturday, and the staff scheduled off for the weekend came to visit Jim and say their goodbyes. It was a very emotional time for everyone. Many tears were shed as they had all become family and had been there for us day and night. The unbelievable level of compassion shown to Jim was inspiring. They each said they would miss his humor, teasing, undying thankfulness, and infectious smile. What an incredible team Jim had at Abbott, and our gratefulness will never fade.

CHOOSE THE CHEESE CURDS

July 3, 2010—new day nine. Discharge day—Praise God. Jim was scheduled to be released early this evening. Before Jim left his home away from home, he asked to go back to ICU. He had made very strong friendships with four other patients waiting for their transplants. Of these four, two of them had gotten their hearts about eight weeks earlier. The third person was the man who had received his heart the same day as Jim. He was the first of the two transplants the team performed that day. The fourth person was in the room next to Jim in ICU, and sadly she was still waiting. She was about half Jim's age and was hanging on until a match could be found. Jim went into her room to say goodbye before we left for home. He told her that her heart would come soon and that we would pray for her. Jim was discharged around 6:30 p.m. We drove straight to our country home and Gunner. Their reunion was extremely wild, and Gunner never left his side. As I said before, Jim had no memory of his cardiac arrest. He lost over two weeks, which is probably for the best. But I told him Gunner was right there on top of him when he collapsed. If dogs could only talk, I can't imagine what

Gunner would say about the last 109 days. They were indeed the best of friends and were forever loyal.

July 4, 2010—new day ten. We spent the entire Fourth of July holiday just relaxing on the deck. It was always a favorite spot of Jim's, and that was all he wanted to do. Our wonderful neighbors, Bill and Karen, visited, and sitting outdoors with them was perfect. Again, these are things that we sadly take for granted. The ability to go outside, sit on the deck, listen to the birds, pet your dog, watch the deer, and enjoy a campfire with great friends are not to be taken for granted. This was all Jim needed to be truly happy. This journey has taught us to be ever so thankful for our big and small blessings. They are all a gift from God, and we should never overlook them. It is such a waste when we miss these gifts right before our eyes, and I can only imagine how sad it makes God. He has provided us with these simple pleasures, but we are too busy to enjoy them. Slow down and enjoy nature—it is a gift from God to be cherished.

We both received another miracle on this day. Just the day before, Jim had told his dear friend in ICU, who had not received her heart yet, that we would pray for her. We got word this afternoon that a match was found earlier this morning, and her transplant was being performed. I tell you, do not underestimate the power of prayer. There are no guarantees that all will be answered, but why wouldn't you ask for help and increase your chances of getting the desired answer? Isaiah 41:10, "So do not fear, for I am with you; do not be dismayed, for I am your God. I will strengthen you and help you; I will uphold you with my righteous right hand." God is good—we must never forget to include Him in our life.

Let's face it—life is hard, very hard. But to have to face it alone is unnecessary, and it must be so overwhelming. God is there just for the asking. He walks beside us and takes our hand on this wild journey called life. I, for one, am terrified of roller coasters. We don't get along with one another. But I could suck it up and go for the wild ride. But I know I will be nauseous and cause myself a fear that would not have happened had I passed on the ride. My second option is to skip the ride and enjoy walking around eating hot dogs, cotton candy, and cheese curds. I alone have the choice to choose my option. I can go with option one and take the wild roller coaster ride and afterward feel like I should be in the fetal position, vomiting. Option two is to enjoy the day eating fun junk food (please don't judge) and watching everyone second-guessing themselves for the roller coaster. I will choose option two all day long. Hopefully, in life, we all choose the option to walk alongside God rather than go it alone on the roller coaster. We aren't always promised cheese curds every day—but walking with God sure beats going through life alone.

OUR NEW NORMAL

July 6, 2010—After resting on July 4 and July 5, we returned to Abbott for a full day of blood tests, scans, exams, and a second biopsy. This would become our new normal for some time. Jim, rightly so, wore his Superman pants to his appointment, and it was so great to see everyone again. It had only been three days, but they had become our family. The staff came to see him wherever his appointments took him around the building. He got a lot of hugs that day, and everyone was so careful in protecting him.

We were learning the utmost importance of keeping Jim away from germs. It was a new concept for us back then wearing a mask. In today's world, not that long ago, it became our only passageway into society. But back in 2010, this was something new for us both. Due to the anti-rejection drugs, Jim would live the rest of his life with a compromised immune system. Keeping germs at bay would become not only innovative but would also be life-saving. I quickly learned a whole new meaning to house cleaning! Before, my concept of cleaning was just to put stuff in less obvious spaces. But at least I never got as bad as a quote I came across recently. "I had to clean my house for two hours just to tell guests—I'm so sorry about the mess!"

We were at the hospital for seven long hours of testing. After returning home, we received a phone call from the transplant team. The biopsy results were in, and Jim's score was zero! Once again, so many prayers were answered, and we told God, "Thank you!"

In our "new normal" life, we were instructed to be very aware of any changes, pain—anything out of the ordinary. Jim was experiencing lower back pain five days later, and Abbott instructed us to go to Monticello Hospital for a blood draw. The results showed some abnormalities, and the transplant team was able to adjust two meds that took care of these latest issues.

When we got back home, Byron was able to help Jim with a problem that was causing his blood pressure to rise. We had put out a new bird feeder, and a raccoon family had discovered it and thought it was for their benefit. Wrong. Jim always loved nature, especially watching the birds, and he was very protective. He wanted no part of sharing the feeder with the recent family of raccoon thieves. But deer, on the other hand, were always allowed to partake.

Biopsies were a big part of the new normal and were performed weekly for the next month. We returned on July 13 for his third biopsy and several tests. While he was waiting for his procedure in the cath lab, a reporter entered his room and asked if they could do an interview. They also had a photographer, and both were from the Minneapolis StarTribune. They spoke with Jim, the staff, and me for nearly forty-five minutes. I remember Jim telling the reporter that he didn't want the article to be about him. But instead, he wanted them to tell the world about all the health professionals who had given him such excellent care and a new lease on life. This included the ambulance drivers that knew us all by our first names, including Gunner, all the staff at Monticello, and the fantastic people at Abbott.

After all his tests were completed, we returned home to rest. A few hours later, we got a phone call from the transplant team. His biopsy results were in, and his score was once again zero! The blessings kept coming, and everything he had gone through brought us to this moment. We were running out of ways to tell God thank you, but we kept trying.

Only a few days later, on July 19, there was a full one-and-a-half-page article with a large picture of Jim lying in his hospital bed. We never expected the article to be this large, and we certainly didn't expect a half-page color photo of Jim, one of his nurses, and me. But to make this even more unbelievable— the article was featured on the front page! Superman had become a legend! One of the state's major newspapers decided to share his story. I recently went online to the archives of the StarTribune and was able to pull up the article. What memories it stirred— some painful and some great.

I remember getting a phone call on the same day the article was published from my brother Lee. They were in Windom at the Dairy Queen when he spotted the StarTribune in a newspaper stand. He called me and said, "Hey, sis, did you know you and Jim are on the paper's front page?" So much for Jim's request not to write the article about him. But rather, the newspaper told Jim's story of the battle he faced and the odds he overcame. We had thought it would be a short paragraph on page four or five. But as in this book, it was hard to write a short story. Jim deserved to have his "fight for life" story told, and I was incredibly happy for him. Just as the newspaper had done, I am doing my best to tell Jim's story because it demonstrates unbelievable faith in God and a determination like none other. My sincere hope is to do his story justice. And just as important, I sincerely hope to help even one person facing struggles coming at them from every direction. You don't have to walk it alone; God is there just for the asking. He will never give up waiting for you—never.

July 21 was Jim's fourth biopsy and a full day of testing. When we walked onto the floor, many staff came running and said, "Superman is in the house!" Of course, he had to wear his Superman pants, which was just a given whenever we returned to the hospital. Later that evening, sitting on the deck at home, we received our phone call again from the team. His biopsy score was zero! I know I sound like a broken record, but that is an excellent thing in this case. We keep giving God our thanks and pray for this broken record to continue.

July 24 was Jim's actual birthday, and he turned sixty-one years old. But we now celebrate it as his one-month birthday. Hard to believe it had already been a month since his gift of life. Mavis gave him a tiny set of porcelain baby shoes to commemorate his new birthday! She had been a rock for us both, and we were so blessed she was in our lives.

Jim and I returned to Abbott on July 28, but this day differed. He had labs, an EKG, a chest X-ray, and several appointments. But today, no biopsy! It was a mixed blessing for Jim. The biopsies were not pleasant procedures, so he was very relieved.

But on the other hand, they had been a sense of security for Jim to know how his body was reacting to its' new organ. They have been tapering down his high dose of anti-rejection drugs every week, so there is naturally some anxiety that his body will continue to accept his new heart. But we followed the doctor's orders, taking his meds and continuing our prayers. We kept hearing the whisper, "I've got this," so there was no reason to doubt it now. Look how far we have come with God leading the way.

August 5 brought us back to Abbott for tests and a fifth biopsy. Jim also attended a support group with people who had already received their gift of life and those still waiting. He was so happy to see two of his 'transplant buddies" there, and they shared their stories. We also got to visit one of his favorites—Vicki. She had walked this journey with us from the first fateful night and was still a tower of strength for us that day. From her bringing puzzles and a table to work them on, hunting magazines, salsa ingredients, and so much more—she was another one of our earthly angels. Once again, later that day, we received a phone call regarding his biopsy. His score was zero! And once again, we heard, "I've got this."

The summer humidity proved to be a challenge for Jim. On humid days, he had to stay inside to help him with his breathing and to prevent any bacteria from thriving in a humid atmosphere. These days were hard on him, as he loved the outdoors. But this was also a new normal for him that needed to happen. You don't make it this far on this journey and take any unnecessary risks. He knew he owed it to the transplant team, the donor's family, and himself to obey the rules.

August 18 was Jim's sixth biopsy, and once again, he received a score of zero. The medical team said he was Superman, as it is not uncommon to see a score of one, depicting mild rejection. After all, a foreign body was implanted in his chest, and his immune system was naturally trained to attack. But with the miracle of his anti-rejection drugs and the expertise of the team—they were able to find just the correct dose to make this balance possible. There was a lot of tweaking and some anxious moments, but with his scores of all zeroes, they knew they were on the right track. Jim and I knew that God—once again—was protecting us both. Whatever the future held—we were so grateful for where we were at that moment.

THE ROAD AHEAD

Jim finally began cardiac rehab at Sister Kenny's outpatient clinic adjacent to the Buffalo hospital. He was scheduled to attend every Monday, Wednesday, and Thursday, concentrating on his muscle tone. He had not regained any of the seventy-one pounds he had lost, so it would be a slow process at each therapy session to rebuild his muscles. In addition, he was given the go-ahead to drive. That greatly helped get him to his appointments, and he was excited to get behind the wheel again. He had not driven since just before the cardiac arrest, so this was a big step forward in his progress. But it also represented something else. His independence had been completely lost since March, and this was a step in regaining it once again.

Jim realized he would have daily hurdles to overcome on his road to recovery, but he faced each day with a positive attitude. We had to make several trips to Abbott because chest pain and blood clots were always threatening. Walking the fine line between anti-rejection drug dosages was always a priority. The organ transplant also messed with Jim's blood sugar. He was not on insulin pre-transplant, but now would be for the rest of his life. He experienced some very dangerous highs and called the transplant team several times. In addition, his magnesium and potassium levels were giving him trouble. It was not an easy road, but this road certainly beat the alternative of not even being alive to fight the fight.

One thing that did not handle this journey well was our garden. With all the appointments, therapy, setbacks, and Jim's lack of strength—the garden became a haven of weeds. The garden was large and now completely overtaken. On the other hand, our German Shorthair, Gunner, loved finding shade in the garden on hot sunny days. One could no longer call it a garden—the term jungle seemed more appropriate. The deer agreed with me, as they would bed there at night for cover. Jim's sister, Carol, was a sweetheart and shared her cucumbers, green beans, tomatoes, and onions with us. We were grateful as this allowed Jim to resume his canning. Without being outside as much as he liked, this gave him a purpose, and he enhanced his canning skills. He prepared us well for the upcoming winter and had much salsa to share.

The end of August brought Jim back to Abbott with chest pains. He had lived most of his life with heart problems, so this was not what he had hoped for at this point in his journey. His doctor at Abbott wanted to admit him to schedule a biopsy and to rule out a blood clot. When his doctor first saw him on the day he was admitted, he said, "Where are your Superman pants?" So, when I returned the following day, Jim got his pants, and all was well again.

This chest pain was a bump in the road. We were gradually getting used to these bumps, and each time Jim became stronger to face the next one. All the trials God puts us through better prepare us for what lies ahead. We did get great news with another biopsy score of zero. Jim remained at Abbott until September 2 to get everything back under control.

Sadly, three days later, he was again admitted to Abbott's ICU. We had a terrifying Saturday afternoon at home and went in around 7:00 p.m. that evening. They were taking him for an MRI and a CT scan later that night. No one had answers but so many questions. Prayers were our lifeline, and we held on so very tight. Infections weren't ruled out, so they began Jim on antibiotics just in case.

The tests all looked good, and the main thing they could contribute was that Jim was dehydrated. This was messing with his magnesium, potassium, and blood sugar. In the past, living with congestive heart failure for so many years—he always had to be careful about his fluid intake. He was still in that mindset after the transplant because that was the life he knew. But now, with a fully functioning heart, he didn't have to restrict fluids. Once his blood tests revealed that he was returning to normal, he was given the green light to return home the following day. Home sounded so good. It had become our favorite place on earth.

Through it all, he still had his sense of humor and thrived again, teasing the staff. He truly missed that aspect of his hundred-plus days there, so he stepped back into his mischief-making role. He was wearing his Superman pajamas and joking with the nurses and doctors. Some nurses had heard of his famous salsa-making skills, so they asked him to write down his recipe. I never looked at what he wrote, but knowing Jim as I did, he probably left out a key ingredient on purpose. He was always having fun and making the most of life, even when life was so difficult. As the saying goes, to not sweat the small stuff—Jim had learned not to sweat the big stuff either. His faith got him through whatever life dealt, and I will always admire him for having that ability. We could all learn from Jim and chill a little.

The following morning when the doctor came into his room, he told him, "Jim, you are normal, or as normal as possible for you!" So, with some medication adjustments, we were on our way home again. I mentioned earlier that I wish Gunner could have talked. I can only imagine what he would have said after all these trips back to Abbott and leaving him home alone. But he, like God and everyone else, never gave up on Jim. We all need to be like our furry friends. They accept us unconditionally and are loyal to the end. God gave us a gift when he created dogs. (Sorry to all you cat lovers out there!)

The remainder of this year consisted of med adjustments, therapy, appointments, and biopsies. This was all part of Jim's "new normal" life. On September 30, October 28, and November 24, Jim had biopsies performed, and each came back with a score of zero. He had gotten perfect scores since his transplant, and there was no explanation other than God whispering, "I've got this."

But as we all know, we are not promised everything we want. We received some devastating news on December 12. My brother, Lee, who had been battling lung cancer for a few years, lost his battle. This was hard for me. I struggled to ask God why he didn't spare Lee's life as he did with Jim's. This is a question to which we will not find an answer while on this earth. But it truly became a time when I had to rely on my faith and God's will. This question would arise many more times in the years ahead and finding peace with it never got easier.

The week of Christmas, Jim again had his monthly biopsy and scored a zero. I was so thankful for this gift but had to come to grips with losing my brother. This year has brought a nearly unbelievable chain of events that I am sure to some sound almost like fiction. But this roller coaster ride happened, and Superman never gave up. We didn't know what the future held, but we were thankful for three things this Christmas. First, the gift of Baby Jesus in the manger, secondly the gift of life given to Jim and third, the gift of our friends and family. It was truly a Merry Christmas as we navigated our "new normal."

FLAMES AND FAITH

Daniel 3:17-18 "If we are thrown into the blazing furnace, the God we serve is able to deliver us from it, and he will rescue us from your hand. O king. But even if he does not, we want you to know, O king, that we will not serve your gods or worship the image of gold you have set up." This verse is the story in the Bible of Shadrach, Meshack, and Abednego. King Nebuchadnezzar summoned them to bow down and worship his gold statue. All three knew the consequences of not bowing down to this earthly king. In Daniel 3:6, we read, "Whoever does not fall down and worship shall immediately be thrown into a blazing furnace."

But the three men remained faithful to God and boldly declared their confidence that God would save them from the fiery furnace. They went on to say *they would not stop serving God even if God didn't save them*. This angered King Nebuchadnezzar so much that he ordered his strongest soldiers to tie them up and throw them into the fiery furnace. He ordered the furnace to be heated seven times hotter than normal for their punishment. The three were bound and thrown into the fire. The flames were so hot that the soldiers were killed instantly after pushing the three men into the flames. In Daniel 3:24-25 we read, "Then King Nebuchadnezzar leaped to his feet in amazement and asked his advisers, "Weren't there three men that we tied up and threw into the fire?" They replied, "Certainly, O king." He said, "Look! I see four men walking around in the fire, unbound and unharmed, and the fourth looks like a son of the gods."

Daniel 3:26-28 (NLT) "Then Nebuchadnezzar came as close as he could to the door of the blazing furnace and shouted: "Shadrach, Meshach and Abednego, servants of the Most High God, come out! Come here!" So Shadrack, Meshack, and Abednego stepped out of the fire. Then the high officers, officials, governors, and advisors crowded around them. Not a hair on their heads was singed, and their clothing was not scorched. They didn't even smell of smoke! Then Nebuchadnezzar said, "Praise to the God of Shadrach, Meshach, and Abednego! He sent his angel to rescue his servants who trusted in him. They defied the king's command and were willing to die rather than serve or worship any god except their own God." The King went on to decree that if any people, no matter their race or nation, spoke a word against the God of Shadrach, Meshach, and Abednego, their houses would be turned into rubble. The King spoke at the end of verse 29 by saying, "There is no other god who can rescue like this!"

As hard as it is, we must have the *"even if He doesn't"* faith. Only God knows the outcome of our daily struggles, but we need to pray and remain faithful no matter what. We may feel like we are walking through fire, but we cannot only have faith when things go our way. We need relentless faith in every situation, just as the three men did, without knowing what will happen next.

February 2011 brought us another huge challenge. Jim was admitted to the ICU at Abbott for fourteen days with sky-high blood pressure, vomiting, headaches, and more. Each time they removed the IV nitro drip, he would elevate to dangerous levels. His blood pressure would easily read 210 over 110. He had now lost another ten pounds during this, and one of his main concerns was that his Superman pajamas were too big and he couldn't keep them from falling down. He never complained about all he was facing but was only worried about his pajama bottoms! Jim had faced battles nearly every day in some form since his transplant. Yet he continued to offer his gratitude to those caring for him. He put his faith in God and never looked back. He faced numerous hospital stays and testing for the remainder of the year.

In March 2012, Jim suffered a nasty fall on the ice in our driveway. I took him to the ER to get checked out. But after he came home again the following morning; he wasn't feeling well. He asked for an ambulance and felt he needed to see the doctor again. There was a terrible snowstorm, and the ambulance couldn't make it down our dead-end gravel road in the country. So once again, the fantastic emergency personnel came to Jim's rescue. The sheriff went to get his four-wheel drive pickup and drove down our road to our house. He helped Jim to his truck and drove the three-quarters of a mile back to the county road where the ambulance awaited. They got stuck once but made it to the Buffalo Hospital after a slow ride. There the staff consulted with the transplant team, and the decision was made to transfer Jim to Abbott for an echocardiogram and a heart biopsy. After testing and overnight stays at Abbott, meds were again adjusted, and Jim returned home…again.

One month later, Jim once again was admitted to Abbott. We had just returned from visiting my family in Arizona. Soon after our trip, Jim got extremely ill with shingles. He was isolated in the hospital and faced huge odds that weren't in his favor. With his reduced immune system, he could not fight the shingle outbreak. They spread so rapidly and covered his face and head. Then they spread into his cornea, where they threatened his eyesight. Jim was critically ill and again faced another struggle for his life. Shingles are serious, but a compromised immune system made this even more critical. They were extremely painful, and his eyes were swollen shut. I thought to myself, "How can this be happening?" All the nearly impossible hurdles this man had jumped, and now stupid shingles may be what brings his life to an abrupt end.

After eight days of pain, dangerously high blood pressure, and desperately trying to save his eyesight—Jim again received a miracle from God and beat the odds. The whisper from God just never stopped, and neither of us had any explanation as to why God would be so kind and generous with Jim's life. The "I've got this" kept presenting itself when Jim faced overwhelming health situations, and it was clear that God wasn't done with him yet. We both were grateful to God beyond words. Upon returning home again, Jim joked that he should change the address on his driver's license to Abbott Heart Hospital. I had to agree, as did the ambulance staff.

In the past few years, we were shown that Jim's transplant came with a price. God had decided to keep Jim on this earth longer, but Jim wasn't promised it would be free from struggles. He would have to face the flames as well. And to put it mildly, the flames sometimes resembled a four-alarm fire! Although his new heart, his gift of life, saved him—he would face many fires because of the transplant.

Our Lord and Savior, Jesus, sacrificed his life for us, which came with a giant price—death on the cross. So, in the grand scheme of things—we both realized that we could handle whatever the price may be - all because of the gift given to Jim. So yes, there have been fires to walk through on this journey. And we know full well that there will be more fires. But we also know we don't have to walk this journey alone. God is there whispering, "I've got this." Deuteronomy 31:6 reads, "Be strong and courageous. Do not be afraid or terrified because of them, for the Lord your God goes with you; he will never leave or forsake you." So, as we walk through the roses and the fire, hold onto your faith. He will choose our path; we will not always understand it or even want to accept it. But in our times of fire, we need to rely on the forgiveness granted to us through His death. In times when we may doubt or question, we can trust knowing we never have to walk this path alone. His right hand is forever present and forever waiting for us to reach up and grab ahold.

OVER AND OVER AND OVER

May of 2012 brought us a brand-new challenge. It was nothing like what Jim had faced up to now. Nothing could have prepared us for the road ahead. Each of the prior challenges had answers on how to manage the challenge. Sometimes it would take time for the medical team to find the answer, but they always did, and Jim managed through and eventually met the challenge. As you know by now—he faced multiple battles, but each time with God's help, he was given the chance to continue his life on Earth.

Joshua 1:9 reads, "Have I not commanded you? Be strong and courageous. Do not be terrified or discouraged, for the Lord your God will be with you wherever you go." Nothing in our life surprises God. He knows every event, every conversation, every happiness, and every sorrow. Our life on this earth will face trials, pain, challenges, and heartaches. But the last part of the verse above is what we must focus on with all our might. "The Lord, your God, is with you wherever you go." This verse has been my brother Wayne's favorite; Jim and I relied heavily on it for strength. Jim had faced so much over the past two years;

hopefully, everything would settle down to our new normal. We both wanted nothing more than to enjoy the new life he had graciously been given.

But...Jim's latest challenge did not have healing solutions like his previous challenges. His new walk through the flames was now facing reoccurring seizures. He was given several neurological tests, and they could only link them back to his cardiac arrest. They felt that his lack of oxygen to the brain back that fateful night in March of 2010 was possibly causing the seizures. No medications were found to bring relief, and the thought of them was always in our minds. Would he suffer a seizure today? Would I be at work, and would he fall from one of these seizures? Knowing that a seizure could come at any moment and being unable to do anything but ride them through was a terrifying thought. The seizures were frightening, and I could only imagine how they made Jim feel. Knowing they were out of his control, just waiting for them to appear, was almost unbearable. It was challenging to hear God's whisper through all this, and Satan was thrilled. After battling these seizures for a month, June brought another set of life-threatening risks.

Jim was discovered to have multiple blood clots in his leg and his lungs. Since the month earlier, he had several trips to Abbott, but now he was admitted beginning a race of time to find the right medications and dosage to dissolve the clots before they moved even closer to the heart. He was also at significant risk of internal bleeding along with the clots.

Each month since the transplant, Jim had faced challenges that would cause anyone else to want to give up. But, as in the past, Jim never wavered, never complained, never gave up, and never lost his faith. Joshua 1:9 was a tower of strength for Jim, and because he knew he wasn't alone, he faced each challenge with an inspiring determination.

As I write this book and relive all Jim went through, I realize God's loving arms surrounded him. No one on earth could handle this alone over and over. Let me repeat myself—no one could do this alone. We are not wired to keep getting knocked down over and over and over. Human instinct would say we've had it, and we're throwing in the towel. But with each "over and over," Jim seemed to become even more determined. He had been given a gift from God with his transplant. An anonymous family had selfishly given Jim their loved one's heart to allow Jim to continue living. But these new health challenges were being blasted at him from all sides. So many times, he wondered if the latest "over and over" would be the one he couldn't overcome. We were both so grateful for each day God had allowed him to continue living, but we faced the reality that these days were numbered. Truthfully, we all face this reality—will today be our last? Or will we be allowed to continue life on this earth and hopefully share the love that God has graciously shown us?

THE THERMOMETER TANKED

Later that same year, Jim received another new challenge. It seemed like there was no end to the "over and over." He was diagnosed with prostate cancer and would require surgery to remove the gland. We had lost count of his "over and overs," but these seemed like our new normal. We wouldn't have picked this as our new normal, but it was the hand we were dealt. Surgery was successful, and he did not require chemotherapy or radiation, which was a big blessing. Once again, Jim beat the odds and realized it wasn't his time to go. It was another instance in his life where God whispered, "I've got this."

Jim did have a big dose of good news in December of 2012. It wasn't medically related, but while hunting at our farm west of Monticello, Jim successfully shot an eleven-point buck. I was working at the time and got a phone call from him. He sounded so out of breath, and my mind immediately took a dark path. But he was sitting on the ground next to the buck. What I thought was out of breath was his excitement for what he had just accomplished. After all this man had gone through the past years—I was so happy for him, and he deserved this win. This single act gave him a dose of the "old normal," which was a blessing. He desperately needed this at a time when "normal" had left his life.

Sadly, this win was soon faced with more challenges. After Jim's prostate cancer, he was diagnosed with two additional cancers over the next year. He was diagnosed with parathyroid cancer, and it was very aggressive. They decided to do two surgeries—one for the parathyroid glands and a second for lymph nodes. Between surgeries, the transplant team scheduled labs and a pre-op physical. This included a stress test to ensure his heart was strong enough for the second surgery. He became ill while taking the stress test, and his blood pressure skyrocketed to 255/155. The test was immediately stopped, and everything was postponed despite the cancer's aggressiveness.

We went back home, but only four days later, Jim was experiencing extreme chest pressure and couldn't get his breath. Once again, we called the ambulance. When they arrived and walked in, they said, "It will be okay, Gunner—we'll take care of him." At this point, I was ready to ask the ambulance team if they could take Gunner and me with them. I didn't think our hearts could take much more stress, either! Jim was rushed to Abbott and administered nitro several times with no success.

He was immediately taken to the cath lab to determine what was happening. Abbott scheduled an angiogram, 2 EKGs, ultrasounds on his legs, and an echocardiogram three days later. The mystery was—why, after seeing all good test results—was this happening? They followed up with an ultrasound of his lungs, looking for blood clots. In addition, a kidney scan was performed because of his high blood sugar. Watching Jim go through all of this made me feel so helpless. The staff felt the same way. I knew by looking into Jim's eyes that he felt this way too. Yes, he had received so many miracles until now, but without us speaking the words out loud, I knew he was thinking what I was thinking. Why Lord? His transplant was supposed to improve his life, but he faced multiple serious complications at every turn.

My mind returned to that November night in 2002 when I begged God to please not give me anymore to handle. I kept these thoughts to myself and tried to show Jim a strong and positive attitude. I knew deep down he was feeling the same way. But I think we each hid our feelings to protect the other. Looking back at this, that was a strong statement of our love for each other. We both tried to shelter one another, but we hid our true feelings by doing so. It felt wrong to be angry with God, although it was hard not to be angry.

This was a point where my thermometer dived downwards. I didn't know how to have the strength to watch Jim suffer through all of this. Of course, this kind and caring man only showed his strength despite how I knew he felt inside. He continued his unwavering genuine compassion for the medical team, trying desperately to find answers. And he kept saying he was worried about me. When all along, I was only worried about him. Why God would allow Jim this much suffering didn't make sense.

Then about an hour later, the unthinkable happened. Jim was lying in his hospital bed feeling ill, and everyone was scrambling to find answers. Then to complicate everything— Jim suffered a horrible seizure. The team came running, and the only way they could get his body to stop seizing was with an injection. I will be bluntly honest—it was challenging to listen for those three words from heaven saying, "I've got this." The whisper couldn't be heard through the noise, chaos, and seriousness. I am sure this is precisely what Satan wanted. He never gives up and waits for a situation like this to take our faith thermometer and plummet it right off the bottom. The one thing I have learned is that Satan never calls a truce. He doesn't give up and looks for any window to sweep in and make us doubt our faith. It felt like Satan was having a loud rock band play at unthinkable decibels to drown out God's whisper. And at this very moment, I desperately needed to hear the whisper.

LET GO

After three days of skyrocketing blood pressure, the transplant team decided to triple all his blood pressure meds. They felt putting his three-year-old heart through these spikes would only end badly. They, at this point, felt it was their only option. In addition to the blood pressure spikes, he struggled with fever, nausea, vomiting, and continued seizures. I knew this latest battle had taken a toll on Jim. For the first time in three and a half years, he did not have the will to joke with the staff. Jim was in so much pain, and his contagious smile had disappeared. Everyone on the staff said they had never seen him like this before. He still wasn't complaining, but he couldn't find the strength or the reason to smile anymore. I feared the worst.

I remember again praying to God and asking, "Why?" Jim had already been through so much, and my human understanding, as limited as it was, questioned God why He would bring Jim this far to watch it all disappear. I know now that this was a normal human reaction, but it was when I needed to take a giant leap forward in my faith. As I said earlier, we want everything according to our plan and timeline. But I needed just to shut up and remember what had gotten us this far. Let go and let God.

I knew if I allowed these feelings of hopelessness to continue, I might be unable to crawl back out of this dark hole. Satan would have such a grip on me, and it would be easy to give up. So, I prayed for strength to face whatever lies ahead. I prayed for Jim not to give up and that God's will be done. This last part of my prayer saved me from abandoning my faith that had brought us both this far. I knew none of this was in our control, and whatever God had planned was His decision, and we needed to accept it with faith. This was not easy, but it was the only way out. I believe that by us *letting go and letting God*, he gave us the strength for another day.

Looking back, I know I have mentioned this before—but Caring Bridge has remained our lifeline to our family and friends. People had gotten used to getting an alert each time I would journal about another challenge Jim was facing. But to have their positive comments and prayers to share with Jim along the way helped bring him hope for what he was facing. Here is an example of the huge outpouring of love and prayers that Jim received. From the day of his cardiac arrest all the way through to his transplant—the first one hundred days of his journey—Jim had 8,210 visits to his Caring Bridge page. He had such a powerful army on his side! Not only was the number of visits to his page incredible, but he also had hundreds and possibly thousands of comments from March through June of that year. These were an incredible inspiration to both of us, and we were so blessed to have this army in our corner. And here we were a few years later, and our family and friends were still following Jim's journey giving their words of hope and comfort.

THE GREATEST GIFT

For obvious reasons, Jim's second cancer surgery was canceled, despite the aggressiveness. After three weeks of constant med adjustments and clinic and lab visits, the team approved his second surgery to complete his parathyroid cancer. It wasn't an easy decision, but the cancer couldn't be ignored any longer and would surely present additional problems if not resolved.

On November 20, 2013, Jim had his second cancer surgery, which went without complications. His heart did great, and the cancer had not spread. I realized the medical science Jim needed for the past month was outstanding and did its' job. The doctors needed to boost his immune system to help keep the cancer at bay. But, in doing so, they risked going too aggressive and allowing the immune system to reject the heart. It was like walking a tightrope, and his doctors were amazing.

Recovery was not a smooth journey. Jim faced elevated blood pressure, fluid retention around the heart, low blood oxygen levels, and pain from the surgery drainage tubes. Once again, Jim was very ill. But he received another miracle from God. He got the news that he would not require chemotherapy or radiation after examining the cancer. He didn't require treatment after his first cancer, and now he didn't again after his second cancer. I was so thankful because we both doubted he could have survived this treatment. Looking back, I am even more thankful, knowing now what I do about cancer treatment and the side effects that unfortunately follow.

Jim was able to make it home in time for Thanksgiving. Unfortunately, in December 2013, he was faced with more challenges. It reminded me of an earlier chapter, "Over and Over and Over." The second drainage tube couldn't be removed because of the large amount of fluid. Right before Christmas, Jim developed a severe infection, causing the team to remove the tube and treat the infection quickly.

Again, we were blessed by my co-workers at Cabela's, our wonderful neighbors, Bill and Karen, helping with Gunner, and another set of dear friends, Eric and Amber, helping with snow removal and delivering delicious home-cooked meals. Despite everything, we again continued to be surrounded by our earthly angels. Our Christmas gift this year was that we had each other, and we had hope for 2014. It was the greatest gift possible, and again, God had whispered.

FIVE HOURS OF JOY

So begins another new year. By now, we had accepted our new normal way of life, not by choice but by necessity. With all the hospital visits, I had to invest in some additional Superman pajama pants, as his earlier ones were getting worn out from all their use! To add to the mix for 2014, Jim had suffered from two torn rotator cuffs from the past year. But given the severity of his other health issues, these were put on the back burner. His right shoulder was determined to be beyond repair and needed a total shoulder replacement. The transplant team felt this was far too risky of surgery, and Jim may not survive. After much deliberation, the decision was made to leave it alone, and Jim endured this pain for the rest of his life.

But they did decide to go ahead with the left shoulder, which wasn't as badly destroyed but was causing severe pain. On April 24, 2014, they performed a left shoulder rotator cuff repair. Once inside, they determined the damage was way more extensive than seen on the MRI. When surgery was completed, he was admitted to the heart hospital so the team could closely monitor him. A pump was inserted to help him handle the surgery pain. After three days, Jim was able to return home. But it was with a needle still in his neck delivering hourly pain medication. The final dose was delivered later that evening. I was given instructions on removing the needle following that final dose. I believe I have been well on my way to a medical degree over the past four years! What I have seen so far is beyond believable. And…we are only four years in!

The following week was difficult, and Jim was again admitted to Abbott. The team recognized the significant deterioration of Jim's strength and his difficulty with the pain. The team came to a necessary but difficult decision. They believed we could no longer care for him at home. Together, side by side, and as a team, we had made it this far. Hearing the words that we were no longer capable of his care was so difficult. We knew they were right, but it didn't make it any easier. It was a huge adjustment for us both.

Jim was transferred that same day to a care facility in Buffalo. Seeing the big bad Superman, who used to drive his Harley in Minnesota on New Year's Eve…now residing in a care facility, broke my heart. He still had a long road of healing ahead, so physical therapy had to be postponed until his recovery was further along. When I returned home later that evening, I felt terrible for Gunner. He couldn't understand why Jim kept leaving home, and I could see it saddened him. I certainly knew how sad it made both Jim and I feel.

Eighteen days later, I arranged for Jim to get a five-hour escape back to our country home. The feeling of joy by both Gunner and Jim was overwhelming. As I mentioned earlier, sadly, we take things for granted. A simple reunion with his dog back home in the country was what Jim desperately needed. We complain over stupid little things when we should pay attention to all the blessings God provides. It can be a simple ray of sunshine, a rainbow after the storm, a letter in the mail from a friend (a lost art, by the way), a hug from someone you love, or a five-hour visit with your dog. These five hours of joy were a blessing and a gift for Jim. Sometimes the best medicine is right in front of our eyes.

The hardest part of this day was driving Jim back to the care facility. But once again, he didn't complain but was more determined to get stronger and return home. He certainly continued to live up to the name of Superman. He had a mission, and eleven days later, on May 31, 2014, he was discharged to return home again. The staff expressed their sadness on seeing him go. They all stated they would miss his great sense of humor and his undying respect for the staff. The one thing that has never changed since 2010 was that Jim bonded with all the medical staff wherever he went. They were as thankful for him as he was for them.

SHINE YOUR LIGHT

We read in Matthew 5:14-15, "You are the light of the world. A city on a hill cannot be hidden. Neither do people light a lamp and put it under a bowl. Instead, they put it on its stand, and it gives light to everyone in the house." I believe Jim was a light for others. When we are in the dark, spiritually or emotionally, we all need light to find our way back. I believe Jim's purpose for surviving these past four years was to provide a light to others. God had plans for Jim and had given him a reason for living. Jim's determination and faith and his "light" led the way giving inspiration to others now and for the future.

We are not meant to hide our lights but to share and shine them for all to see. As it goes on in Matthew 5:16, "In the same way, let your light shine before men, that they may see your good deeds and praise your Father in heaven." This had become Jim's mission given by God. Although Jim had to face enormous trials and suffering to be able to shine, he did so at every turn and with no complaints. We all have the mission to be a light for a troubled world. Let your light shine as Jim did. We owe this to God…and I owe it to Jim.

Jim did get diagnosed with a third cancer over the past year, but this one was not delivering the complications the others had posed. He had been diagnosed with skin cancer, and while some proved to be minor, some were more severe and required surgery. We kept a close watch on him, and whenever something was seen as suspicious, he would go to his dermatologist to take care of it quickly. It would be another "over and over" as he battled skin cancer many times over the following years.

I want to take this opportunity to thank all of you who were so kind to purchase my book. I have never done this before, but I have this strong sense of the Holy Spirit guiding me as I write each page. This book is causing me to relive everything we went through. But I am receiving an unexpected gift through this process. As I refer to my printed book from my Caring Bridge journals, I relive all the love shown to us by our friends and family in their comments. It has helped me more than I could have imagined as I am writing about the painful memories of Jim's health journey. With each new challenge, I sadly remember how much pain Jim endured. But, with love and admiration, I recall how strong, determined, and faith-filled he was. God was allowing Jim's light to shine for others to see, and hopefully, it also strengthened them. There is a lesson for us all during the dark times that we will undoubtedly face. This lesson is to do our best not to hide in the darkness but seek God and His light. By doing so, our light will shine, and just as with Jim—we can provide a guiding light for others to follow.

BITTERSWEET

In August 2014, together, we made a tough decision. We were leaving our country home, which had become our sanctuary. We had lived there for seven years, and it was our constant source of peace. Plus, we had the blessing of our neighbors, who helped us through so much. Jim's health had seen numerous ambulance rides, countless hospital stays, appointments, scans, and blood draws over the past four and a half years. Because of this, we reluctantly decided to move closer to Abbott and all the services his health demanded. It was a bittersweet decision and one not taken lightly. Our hearts said to stay in the country, but our heads told us to move closer to the hospital.

On September 1, 2014, we moved in with my son, Jason, relocating to Blaine, MN. This was only about twenty minutes from Abbott and helped lessen some of the fears we faced earlier with being so far away. In keeping with tradition, Jim was introduced to the Blaine ambulance crew six days after we moved. It was September 7, 2014, and Jim collapsed in the parking lot at Walmart. I stayed with him on the ground until the ambulance arrived, and they took him to a local hospital for an overnight stay. He was sent home with a forty-eight-hour heart monitor to record if there were any more severe drops in his blood pressure. Little did the Blaine ambulance crew know how well they would get to know us.

Moving forward to March 24, 2015—Jim was again transported by ambulance to Mercy Hospital in Coon Rapids. He had stroke-like symptoms, and although we wanted to go to Abbott, they had to transport him to the closest hospital because of the severity. They were unfamiliar with Jim's health history, so I tried to get them up to speed. They could see his chart in the Allina health system, but by now, it was like reading War and Peace. It was so lengthy, and no doctor would ever have or take the time to read it from beginning to end. They discovered multiple blood clots in his lungs but didn't feel these were causing the intense headaches and loss of speech he was experiencing.

They scheduled an MRI later that evening to rule out a possible brain mass. Jim somehow found the strength between his attacks to joke with the staff. But he would be in so much pain during the attacks that he just lay there and suffered. Five days later, it was now March 29, and still no answers. After another two days, they decided to taper back his seizure meds. Over the years, doctors have continued to increase his dose as he continued to battle the seizures. But now, reviewing this, they have concluded that the seizure medication at this high dose could be causing the seizures.

They continued to treat him for blood clots while slowly tapering his seizure meds. Once again, Jim's strength had diminished, and he was not strong enough to return home. He was transferred to a rehabilitation center in Anoka, about twelve miles away. His progress there would determine his length of stay. They initially anticipated a thirty to sixty-day hospital stay to regain strength and to continue the schedule of tapering his seizure meds. We both did our very best to stay positive with this latest hurdle. All I could think was this poor man needed a break.

Jim, aka Superman, ended up beating the odds again, and his determination to get stronger outweighed their estimation of how long he would be there. His stay lasted three weeks, and he was discharged on April 14, 2015. He would continue physical therapy with a home therapist. In addition, a home health nurse came periodically to monitor his INR levels for his blood thinner medication. The bittersweet decision to move to Blaine proved best for Jim's health. All these facilities were nearby, and the numerous resources necessary for his in-home care were provided.

When Jim returns home, you can only imagine how Gunner feels. He was so happy but also confused. Jim came home with a walker, and tennis balls were on the legs to help slide it along the floor. Gunner couldn't understand for the life of him why he wasn't allowed to play with these balls. Also, as I mentioned earlier, we had moved in with my son. He also had a dog, and his name was Barney. Barney was just as excited to see Jim; now, both dogs thought the tennis balls were for them and them alone.

NOT PREPARED FOR THIS ONE

In the months ahead, 2015 brought a whole new and unexpected challenge—no way we were prepared for this one. We were doing okay handling the home rehabilitation for Jim, and my continued role as his caregiver was happening with no bumps in the road. The past five years have become our new way of life. I was Jim's caregiver and advocate whenever we went for doctor appointments, labs, or hospital visits. His health history was so long and complicated that I would summarize for them his medical history up to that point. The other alternative was for them to read his MyChart medical records, but that had become so time-consuming. One doctor said he had never seen a longer medical record in his career, and it would be impossible to read it in under three or four hours. I was used to this role and had no problem providing them with this summary. It gave Jim and me a sense of peace and gave the doctors a thorough understanding of Jim's health.

Fast forward to Friday, June 26, 2015— I was scheduled for my annual mammogram. They are always such a joy and something every woman looks forward to with great anticipation. Please know that I am being sarcastic…very sarcastic! It was not enjoyable and something I dreaded. That morning my two dear friends, Jaqui and Chy, unaware of my appointment, reached out and wanted to meet for lunch. I remember telling Jim I would cancel my appointment and meet them instead. A delicious lunch with best friends versus a mammogram. Hmm…it was an easy choice to make. Lunch it was!

To this very day, I can still hear Jim's voice when I tell him of my changed plans. He replied, "Sure, don't go - get cancer and die!" Jim always was one to say what was on his mind, and he did this day. It was harsh to hear, but the kick in the butt was precisely what I needed. So, I put on my big girl pants, skipped lunch, and attended my appointment. Afterward, I thought, "Well, I've done that for another year!"

With the appointment on a Friday, the nurse told me I would get my results back on Monday. I had countless mammograms in the years past—fifteen to be exact. I expected this one to go smoothly as well. On Sunday evening, out of curiosity, I checked my health record in MyChart to see if the results were in yet. When I opened the file on my computer, all that came across the top of the page was one word. Abnormal. I read their brief notes about a mass and knew I would get a phone call early Monday morning. By 8:00 a.m. that next day, I received a call from them asking me to schedule a second mammogram for the following day at the imaging center.

So not only did I have to repeat the fun-filled mammogram, but I now also had to worry about the mass. But even more present in my thoughts was something different. I had spent the last five years being the one who was the caregiver. Facing the possibility of being the one who needed to be cared for scared me to death. The only thought that night was that I couldn't possibly be sick. I needed to care for Jim and couldn't let anything get in my way.

For the remainder of the evening, my mind went to dark places. All the faith-filled days of the prior years seemed so far away. I tried my best to stay positive but felt my thermometer sliding downwards. I did my best to put up a brave front, more for Jim than myself. But I knew very well that Jim was scared too. We had traveled hand in hand all these years, and now again, we faced the possibility of losing our partner. First, I had faced that possibility for the past five years, but now the roles were reversed. Now Jim had to face the possibility of losing me.

Jim had a heart of gold, and I knew he was questioning if he could take on the caregiver role. I knew he wouldn't *hesitate a second* to try and care for me. But we both were facing the question without saying it out loud…, would he be healthy enough to help me face this battle and provide the required care. To complicate everything, he would need to face his health without my caregiving. It was a dark cloud that I knew loomed so heavily over the both of us.

I did not sleep that night. As I had done in the past, I asked God why? We had been faithful through everything thrown at us and faced yet another storm. Jim's light had shone over the past five years and inspired others. Now I wondered if my light was growing dim.

I CHOOSE OPTION TWO

Psalm 62:2 reads, "He alone is my rock and my salvation; he is my fortress, I will never be shaken." Life can throw us curve balls, and we don't always handle them the best. We ask why and feel that we don't deserve this. This was true in this case. We had been through so much, and now another mind-numbing issue was facing us right between the eyes. But life is difficult, and the Bible does not suggest otherwise. We get the option to walk it alone or walk it with God.

I drove to the imaging center for my second mammogram the following day. I sat alone in the waiting room, feeling my faith thermometer tanking. But at the same time, I could hear a whisper from God saying, "I've got this." Both the Lord and Satan were fighting for my attention that day. It felt like a tug of war inside my body. Each was pulling me in their direction, and I faced two options. Option one was the easy path. This is where I would be angry with God and let Satan take me to that dark hole. Option two was the difficult path. I could choose to stay strong in my faith and take my own advice—let go and let God. *I chose option two*. I prayed for God to walk alongside me on this journey, wherever it would take me. Once again, Satan retreated as the loser of this battle. But trust me, he always tries again, and he'll be back. We must always be ready to recognize him and send him packing.

Once the mammogram was completed, I was asked to wait while a doctor reviewed the results. I was called back into his office, and he asked if I could stay longer so they could perform an ultrasound to get a closer look. I wanted answers as much as they did, so I agreed. Once the ultrasound was done, I was again called back into the doctor's office, and he asked if I could come back four hours later for a biopsy. He said all the tests looked suspicious, and a biopsy was needed to confirm. I drove home for a few hours and tried to keep my mind from worry overload. I returned a little later, and they performed a biopsy on my right breast. They informed me I would be getting a call either way, the next day.

Everyone has heard the phrase that God won't give you more than you can handle. I remember praying that night that the test would be negative, and that Jim and I could return to everyday life. We were as far from normal as anyone could be —but it was our normal. With this prayer, I didn't even realize what I had just done. I asked God for everything to work out as I wanted. You would have thought I would have learned this by now with everything we had been through. But obviously, my fear took over, and I prayed for the desired result and didn't consider what God wanted.

My phone rang on Wednesday, July 1, 2015, at 2:10 p.m. I remember walking out to the garage to take the call. I wanted to be alone when I heard the results, no matter what they were. Also, I wanted to protect Jim from seeing my face if I didn't get the news I had hoped for. I answered the phone, and the nurse on the line asked if this was Trudy, and I answered yes. The following words were, "I'm so sorry, but you have cancer." No one, absolutely no one, is ever prepared to hear those words. I remember thinking so many thoughts, all racing at once. How can I tell Jim? How can I tell my kids? I wished my mom was still here because I needed her right then. How serious is this, and did we catch it soon enough? How could God allow this beast of disease to invade my body? My mind was swirling like a floodgate that had just been opened wide.

I was diagnosed with triple-negative breast cancer. I was told it is an extremely aggressive type of breast cancer, and treatment is not always successful. The tumor was embedded deep in the dense tissue so that self-examination couldn't feel it. It was over 2 cm, and the ultrasound revealed invasive ductal carcinoma with lymphovascular invasion.

My cancer was labeled stage two. Stages of cancer speak to how advanced the cancer is and range from a score of zero to four. With triple-negative breast cancer, it is imperative to determine the grade of cancer as well. To further evaluate, the grade of breast cancer measures the aggressiveness and the rate of tumor growth. To get technical with you, there is a scoring system called the Nottingham score which determines the grade or aggressiveness.

This test looks at the breast cancer cells under a microscope and rates the tumor on three criteria. The score ranges from a minimum of three to a maximum score of nine. The low-end score of three indicates a tumor much less aggressive. A score of eight or nine indicates a much more aggressive and fast-growing tumor. In addition, it is seen as a higher risk of recurrence. My Nottingham score was a nine. That is not good news. This was a lot of big words that were hard to hear, let alone understand. With triple-negative breast cancer, if *one does survive*, the life expectancy is typically not long. In addition, in many cases, this type of cancer will reappear in only a year. Because of this grade score of nine, they set up appointments immediately as time was not on our side. At this moment, I had Jim to thank for not choosing lunch with my friends!

Jim took the news hard but was determined to help me through this to the best of his ability. He put all his pain and health issues on the back burner to walk with me on our latest journey. I remember feeling just as bad for him as I felt for myself. It was clear that option two of turning over our latest challenge to God would be a difficult road ahead. There would be days when we would continue to ask why. But I couldn't even imagine making it a single day by choosing option one. I will always be grateful that God is forever ready and waiting for us to choose option two.

The following week was hectic—more ultrasounds, X-rays, MRIs, and blood work, to name a few. An appointment was set with a surgeon. Jim was not physically strong enough to accompany me, and I knew it tore him up inside. But my dearest friends, Jaqui and Chy, went with me for moral support. They both helped me through a difficult appointment, and surgery was to be scheduled in two weeks. The wait was due to no current openings in his surgery schedule. As scary as it was, I remember thinking I want this thing out of me now! I remember clearly when my mom was diagnosed with cancer; she said the same thing. Knowing cancer is inside you is awful, and you want it removed as quickly as possible. The doctor discussed the possibility of a lumpectomy as opposed to a mastectomy. I wanted no part of this. These things were trying to kill me, and I wanted them gone.

After the surgeon's appointment, my dear friends drove me to have fun and take my mind off everything. We ended up at the casino, laughed, had fun, and ate ice cream. For a short while, I forgot what I was about to face. We have a photo from that day of the three of us eating our ice cream cones with big smiles. It was a great memory; to this day, it is one of my favorite pictures. I don't remember if we were lucky or not on the slots, but it didn't matter. My friends had given me a priceless gift - a special day to treasure and to draw on its memory in the difficult road ahead.

I had done so much research over the past week to understand the battle I faced. It was not going to be easy fighting this very aggressive cancer. My cancer type did not respond to hormone therapy, and my tumor was already large. But plans changed abruptly once the doctors returned my MRI results. In one week, the tumor had doubled in size, and the decision was quickly made to move immediately to chemo and put surgery on the back burner. There wasn't time to perform the surgery and wait for recovery before beginning chemo. The MRI results cast a dark shadow over my diagnosis and clearly showed that time was not on our side. Satan reappeared and tempted option one to me again, as I knew he would. But I held strong, not by my strength, but by God's strength, and I remained steadfast with my choice of option two.

BELIEVE

My dear brother, Wayne, sent me an inspiring card soon after my diagnosis. It was a Hallmark card, so I need to credit them for the beautiful words written. The front of the card reads like this:

I know God works in mysterious ways,
but sometimes, I wish He'd let us in
on His thinking a little more.
Like why you are having to go through
what you're going through right now?
It sure can't be explained by our human-sized logic.
I know He has a master plan, and I know that good
can come out of what we see as bad, but still…
I know you're hurting, and my heart hurts for you.
So, I want you to know I'm praying for you
and asking God to nurture you and hold you in His hands.

He wrote on the inside of the card:
You'll get through this. I believe it. I do.

The word *"Believe"* became my go-to word of encouragement and hope through my cancer journey. To this day, it is still my "word" that gets me through the day.

On July 10, 2015, I met with my oncologist. I had never had an oncologist before, and they assigned me one for my treatment. It turned out to be a divine intervention. My oncologist was terrific; I couldn't imagine going through this with any other doctor. It was determined I would begin an intensive chemotherapy treatment. The two beginning chemo drugs were powerful and could damage the heart. Because of this, they did an echocardiogram to ensure my heart could withstand the treatment. Also, because of this, I now had an additional doctor—a cardiologist that would monitor my heart throughout my treatment. This type of chemo would give me the best chance at stopping this aggressive cancer. But as with any medicine, it came at a cost. It would also bring on the strongest side effects as well.

After getting the go-ahead from the cardiologist, I went to the hospital on Tuesday, July 14, to have a port inserted into my chest. This was where the chemo and all future blood draws would be administered. The port also helps by not having to use your veins and risk them collapsing over time. Another dear friend of mine, Natalie, took me to this appointment. I'll admit things were all moving so fast, and I was so scared. The procedure was excruciating, and I shed many tears. When I was finished, it was a Godsend to have Natalie there for support and to drive me home. She had a powerful faith, and I drew on that to get through the day.

The following day, Wednesday, July 15, I returned to my oncologist to double-check my blood work. My dear friends, Jaqui and Chy, were with me, and I couldn't be more thankful.

Listening to chemo's side effects the day before was enough to send one over the edge. The list included: anemia, appetite changes, bleeding, constipation, diarrhea, fatigue, flu-like symptoms, fluid retention, weight gain, hair loss, infection, mouth and throat sores, metallic taste in the mouth, nausea and vomiting, nervous system changes, pain, skin/nail changes, eye changes and finally, urinary, kidney and bladder changes. I thought to myself, "Oh good, sign me up!"

Everyone reacts differently to chemo, and even though it was so scary, I wanted to know what lies ahead in just a matter of a day. The doctors prescribed five different medications to help with the side effects and some to keep my blood counts from dropping too low. To anyone who has experienced cancer and treatment, I admire your strength. I prayed for that same strength now.

My blood work looked good, and it was a go for chemotherapy to begin. As Jaqui, Chy, the oncologist, and I walked to the infusion room, I was unprepared for what I saw. There were about six rows of recliners with patients sitting there cuddled with blankets and multiple IVs hooked up to their ports. Everyone was at different stages in their treatment. Some had gone through several weeks and looked so pale and tired. Many had lost their hair, and some even the will to live. I remember clearly nearly all of them looking at me with the same emotion on their faces—a feeling of pity. They knew full well what was ahead for me, and they could feel my fear. Some were alone with no family or friends sitting by their side. I couldn't even imagine that, and I was so thankful for my friends that I couldn't even find the words. At this very moment, I had to dig deep into my soul and repeat the word "Believe" while straining to hear God whisper, "I've got this."

My port had just been installed the day before and was still very painful. The need for treatment to begin immediately was necessary, and it was decided the first treatment would be done intravenously instead. A good vein could not be found after a few unsuccessful painful pokes in my arm. The RN then proceeded to administer the chemo in my port. With a pain-stricken face and tears rolling down my cheeks, I knew this was now a reality as my treatment began. They also administered three additional anti-nausea medications and a steroid as the road ahead was about to get bumpy.

After hours of treatment, my friends and I met with the RN Coordinator, and I was shown head dressings and wigs. The effects of my chemo had not hit me yet, and I remember one incident that brought laughs to us all. One of the wigs I tried on made me look exactly like Mrs. Doubtfire! Even in this time of fear, God had given us this moment of laughter. There were also training and DVD educational information, as well as pamphlets to read. We also met with the oncologist and discussed financial resources and locating local support groups for people living with cancer. By now, I was beginning to feel the effects of this day, leaving me in an emotional state of exhaustion and fear. My day ended with fatigue, nausea, pain, no appetite, and many tears. So many, many tears.

I was given several medications to take at home until I returned for my next round of chemo. These included additional nausea meds, prednisone, and strong pain meds. I also received a self-administering unit with a small needle to insert into my arm the following morning. This was to help my white count from dropping to dangerously low levels. It was almost too much to handle. I remember how helpless and sorry Jim felt for me. Here he was faced with his own health problems, and he was worried about me. It was so difficult for me as well, not being able to care for him as I had done for so many years. We both struggled with our feelings and what we were facing. It just didn't seem fair. But no one is ever promised fair.

SENDING UP A SMOKE SIGNAL

Going through some old boxes the other day, I came across a short reading that an Arizona employee and friend of mine, Maggie, had given to me. She wanted me to share the reading with an elderly employee on my team who had just lost his wife. This simple piece of paper from over twenty years ago was appropriate today. I do not know who penned this writing, but I want to share it now.

The only shipwreck survivor was washed up on a small, uninhabited island. He prayed feverishly for God to rescue him, and every day he scanned the horizon for help...but none seemed forthcoming. Exhausted, he eventually managed to build a little hut out of driftwood to protect himself from the elements, as well as to store his few possessions.

One day, after scavenging for food, he arrived home to find his humble little hut in flames, with smoke rolling up in the sky. The worst had happened, and everything was lost. He was stunned with disbelief, grief, and anger. "God, how could you do this to me?" he cried. Early the next day, he was awakened by the sound of a ship approaching the island. It had come to rescue him. "How did you know I was here?" asked the weary man of his rescuers. They replied, "We saw your smoke signal."

It's easy to get discouraged when things go wrong, but we shouldn't lose heart. God is at work in our lives, even amid pain and suffering. So, remember the next time your little hut seems to be burning to the ground - it just may be sending the smoke signal that summons the grace of God. The reading ended with these wise words: You may want to consider passing this on because you never know who feels like their hut is on fire today.

Today I knew God had seen my smoke signal that first night of my chemo treatment. I was in a dark place and felt so alone. But God saw the smoke and came to my rescue. He also sent me his earthly angels to help put out the fire. With all the support from my family and friends, it felt like I had an entire fire department rescuing me from my "fire and smoke," once again, God had amazed me.

I was fortunate to have Jaqui enter Caring Bridge updates for all my friends and family. There was no way I had the strength to do this, and she kept people up to date on my journey. Their prayers and words of support meant the world to me. It helped tremendously knowing that I wasn't walking this journey alone. In addition, Jaqui and Chy began a planner on my Caring Bridge page and entered requests for help. It included anyone who wanted to deliver meals, get Jim to his appointments, or anything else he may have needed. Jim, although he couldn't physically help with my care, I knew his prayers and support were so genuine, and he was a big part of my "fire department."

I thought the first three days following my first treatment were the worst. I was, unfortunately, wrong. The fourth day was excruciating. I was experiencing so much fatigue, but the prednisone gave me insomnia at night. I also suffered from extreme heartburn and felt like I had an all-over sunburn—but from the inside out. My treatment regimen consisted of Cytoxan and Adriamycin. The latter of the two is called the "red devil." It got this name for several reasons. First, it is red, but it is also very toxic. It can cause cardiac damage and is very caustic, causing severe burns if it touches your skin. In addition, I was told to flush the toilet twice each time in the days following treatment! What the heck??!! This is so the toxins my body released couldn't be spread as quickly. NONE of this was comforting and seemed so hypocritical that you must inject your body with poison to get well?!?

As sick as I felt, I think my entire body emitted smoke signals from every crevice. If ever I needed God, it was now. Jim had to be hospitalized for stomach pain and abdominal bruising in the next few days. How could this be happening? As I knew I would, I felt so guilty not being able to help him as I had in the past. I was so sick, but as I viewed it, I had abandoned Jim by being unable to help him through his latest health struggle. This made me very sad and very helpless.

On July 27, 2015, I returned to my oncologist, who examined the incision on my chest where my port had been implanted. It was red, and they feared infection. I was put on a ten-day dose of antibiotics. My white count was normal after my first treatment, so they scheduled my next chemo dose. It was so discouraging that just as you begin to feel better, you go back and start all over again. But this would have to happen if I would beat this monster. I was already beginning to see a little of my hair falling out. There is no possible way one can be prepared for this. I, for years, had long, thick hair, and now it was being taken away by the chemo. I couldn't handle the thought of huge chunks of hair on my pillow in the mornings, so I made a hair appointment to cut it and go very short. I will never forget seeing the piles of hair on the salon floor, knowing what was coming next. This was another time when I was sending up a smoke signal for help.

On July 29, I returned to the infusion lab and began round two of the "red devil." By now, I had begun seeing more of the side effects that this poison causes. After this treatment, large amounts of hair were on my pillow the following day. I can't imagine what it would have been like if I hadn't just gone and gotten it cut. So, my first look in the mirror that day was a half-bald head, a puffy face from the prednisone, and a feeling of nauseousness from all the meds. I got so angry with the chunks of hair falling out that I borrowed Jim's razor and said, "Okay….take that @#$! cancer!" I shaved my entire head while tears were falling down my face. So many smoke signals begging for help.

COMFY QUILT

By now, my Caring Bridge pages were filling up with words of encouragement from so many friends and family. As sick as I was and unable to get out of bed, the messages from everyone kept me going more than they would ever know. As I lay there and read each one, I managed to do a journal entry. I wrote that I had realized that all the paths I had crossed since childhood were becoming a "weaving" from the Lord. It began in my hometown of Storden; then to California, Spicer, Pennsylvania, Arizona, and back to Minnesota. From Monticello, to Rogers, and finally Blaine—everyone along this lifelong journey had positively impacted my life. These paths were all being "woven" by God into a huge comfy quilt, wrapping me with warmth and love while holding me safe during this cancer journey. Knowing I wasn't in this battle alone brought me comfort. God had provided *everyone to be woven into my life and now had reunited us all* on Caring Bridge. He works in such amazing ways. Little did I know that as I met each of these people earlier in my life, they would bring me such support, prayers, and love now when I needed it most. To this day,

I am so very thankful for each one of them for being woven into my human "comfy quilt" by our Lord and Savior. It made me weep when I read one of the Caring Bridge entries from a dear friend, Amber. She wrote, "YOU are our comfy quilt."

Round two of the "red devil" lived up to its' name. I was so weak that just walking across the room was a struggle. I now had the metallic taste in my mouth they warned of, and nothing I ate or drank tasted good. My "comfy quilt" was about to get even more comfy as my daughter, Melissa, was flying in the next day from Phoenix. I hadn't seen her since my birthday in February, when I flew out and had the absolute joy of helping her pick out her wedding dress. The wedding was scheduled for March 2016, and I planned to beat this cancer and enjoy her wedding day with our family.

My daughter flew in on August 5, and we had the best time together, even though I was still sick. On the evening of August 6th, she went to spend some time with her brothers, and Jim and I stayed home. I began feeling a little feverish and was starting to experience pain. I phoned the on-call nurse and told her of my symptoms. She said I needed to go immediately to ER, given that I had experienced that infection in my port earlier. I told her I had an appointment with my oncologist the following day, so I thought I would wait until then to be seen. The on-call nurse disagreed and thought I should be seen now to be safe. After hanging up, I told Jim about the conversation, and his words were simple…" *listen to the nurse!*" Once again, his words were great advice.

I was shocked at how quickly I was becoming more ill. The antibiotic dose I had been on had somewhat kept the infection at bay, but as soon as the ten-day dosage was over—the infection went wild. Since my kids were all gone for the evening and Jim could not drive—I got in the car and drove myself to the ER. From the first minute they saw me—everything moved so quickly. My fever had spiked, and my white count had tanked. My port site in my chest was so red, and they knew immediately the antibiotic I had been given had not taken care of the infection. They discovered that I had pancytopenia after getting the blood work results back.

This is a condition where the body has dangerously low levels of red blood cells, white blood cells, and platelets. The red cells carry oxygen to all your organs and tissues. White cells help your body fight infection; clearly, they could not handle whatever was raging war with my body. Platelets stop bleeding when you are cut or injured. With all three of these severely compromised, the medical team diagnosed me with sepsis. This is a life-threatening emergency caused by your body's overwhelming response to an infection where the body begins causing injury to its tissue and organs. Without urgent treatment, it can lead to tissue damage, organ failure, and death within hours.

I was now already in kidney failure, and the doctors quickly realized the severity of what we were facing. I was rushed to a hospital room and immediately began taking broad-spectrum antibiotics. Very early the following day, I was sent down to surgery to get my port removed. The infection had traveled the length of the port and was poisoning my body. I'm unsure why…but they did the procedure while I was awake. The pain I was already experiencing at the port site and this port removal was almost unbearable. They did numb the site, but it hurt so much that I lay there and cried. The broad-spectrum antibiotics were to be given until the cultures could be grown for forty-eight hours to identify what was causing the infection that had taken over my body.

I was so scared, and the realization had now sunk in. The doctors informed me what would have happened if I had not come into ER that night, but instead waited for my appointment the following day. They said another twelve hours of no treatment would have allowed the bacteria to cause far more damage and most likely would have been fatal overnight. More than likely, I would not have even woken up to make my morning appointment! These conditions, especially sepsis, move at an alarming rate throughout the body, and with a diminished immune system due to chemo and pancytopenia—I would not have survived. In a matter of six weeks, Jim helped save my life twice, as I had saved his five years earlier. He is the one that made me go to my mammogram rather than lunch with Jaqui and Chy. Now he was the one who told me to listen to the overnight nurse and NOT to wait until the following day. Thank you, Jim—you saved my life.

Over the next three days, the infection did not respond to the antibiotics. The meds were helping the infection to not spread but was not treating it. When the results of the culture came in, they realized what they suspected was not the case. They had thought it was a staph infection, but it was a deadly bacteria called pseudomonas aeruginosa. The biggest danger of this strain of bacteria is that it can lead to high mortality because it can be very drug resistant. They immediately changed course and put me on what they called their most powerful antibiotic known. Now all we could do was wait and see if the damage could be reversed.

Along with the hospital's heated blankets, I was even more thankful for the warmth of my "comfy quilt" from everyone on Caring Bridge and for friends and family who visited. As I mentioned earlier, every single one of these people had been woven into my life over the years—all part of God's plan. My time with each of these people had been such a blessing. But I didn't see the big picture that God saw. He knew that one day I would need an army to cheer me on for this battle. And again, after reading the comments in Caring Bridge, I knew just how blessed I was with everyone's support. From the bottom of my heart, I thanked God for my "comfy quilt." It was His gift when I needed all the comfort I could get.

Many doctors and tests happened over the next few days to closely watch if the antibiotic was healing the infection. Also, I was scheduled for an ultrasound to see if my tumor had shrunk. I had been scheduled for round three of chemo, but that was pushed back one week to better heal from this massive bump in the road. Thankfully after five days, I was discharged on August 11. I remember so clearly that it was the same day my daughter was flying back home to Phoenix. We told the nurse that we only had ten minutes to complete the discharge so that Melissa could make her flight. They all ran around like they had eaten ten doughnuts and washed them down with four cups of coffee! One gave us the meds to take home, another gave us the discharge papers with instructions, and another ran to get a wheelchair to get us to the front entrance. I had been through so many hospital discharges with Jim, and they are NOT a quick process. This one was a discharge for the record book. And we made her flight in time! I heard God's whisper that day, "I've got this!" Like Jim had many times before, I beat the odds and was so glad to return home to him.

A few days later, I got the great news from the ultrasound that my tumor had shrunk 25 percent. The "red devil" was so hard on my body, but it worked against the monster inside me. God had again, for the millionth time, answered prayers. We were on the right track; this bump in the road was behind us, and we could move forward with round three of chemo. I was slowly getting my strength back, and my blood levels were beginning to rise again. Even though I knew the next round of chemo would take them back down again, I was ready for the challenge. Today the quilt felt even more comfy and warm.

THIS TOO SHALL PASS

Chemotherapy resumed on August 21, 2015. This brought a new set of complications. At this point, I almost expected them and wondered how I would beat them. I had begun to have a low-grade fever and had some intestinal problems. Okay, to be honest—good ol' diarrhea. I was sick from my third round of treatment, but the lab needed a stool sample to determine the newest infection. This is where my dear friend, Jaqui, stepped in and did the unthinkable. She went above and beyond and came to my home to pick up the stool sample and deliver it to the hospital. Not everyone would be willing to transport a stool sample in their car—let alone one that wasn't theirs! I don't think too many people would jump up and down and say, "Pick me! I'll deliver your poop!" But she did and later told me she even buckled it with the seatbelt in her car. I'm sure she didn't want this "passenger" to be able to move around! The call came later that I had a new infection to face. I had C diff, also known as clostridioides difficile. It is a bacteria caused by antibiotics in your system that destroy the good bacteria in your colon. Since I had several weeks of antibiotics, this complication was a real possibility, and here it was. So, now we began treating that and coping with the chemo side effects. But by now, another new motto of mine was....this too shall pass. At this point, I was only nine days out from my fourth chemo treatment, so the days ahead would be challenging.

God gave me the strength to get through this phase, and on September 2, I received my fourth round of chemo. As I said, some nicknamed this chemo the "red devil.' By now, however, I had other names I had given my treatment. I would love to share them with you, but probably leave them to your imagination to give me a better chance at publishing my book! I now had reached day sixty-five of my journey and have been given a two-week time off to recover. Then I would begin phase two of my chemo treatments. Thankfully I am done with the "red devil" and will move on to another chemo named Taxol. Unfortunately, round four proved too much for my body to handle. My energy level had gotten so low that I would instantly get short of breath if I walked a few steps.

I had now developed a fever of 102 and was again admitted to the hospital. My lab work showed that my white blood count had dropped to 0.5, and I was severely neutropenic. Neutrophils are white blood cells produced in the bone marrow and ingest bacteria. They comprise about 60 percent of all white blood cells and play a key role in the body's defense. Neutropenia is an abnormally low concentration of neutrophils. This condition can occur between seven and twelve days after one receives chemotherapy. I was in isolation in the hospital because I had no immune system. I was given a blood transfusion, and after a few days of blood counts rising and thirty-six hours with no fever— I was given the green light to return home. It had been a rough four days, and I didn't ever want to feel that sick again.

In a song by Larry Fleet labeled "This Too Shall Pass," the words bring comfort to anyone facing a battle. The most significant message from the song for me is that I am not alone, He hears my prayers, and He knows my name.

Back at home, all I did was rest. My body had been beaten, and I needed to regain strength to prepare for round two of my chemo regimen. My oncologist pushed my treatment back another week to give me more time to get stronger. Re-reading my Caring Bridge journal, I wrote that I was happy to have the break. I went on to say, "Besides that…I need a week to recover from the Vikings game!" Looking back on Google, I see that we lost to the 49ers by a score of twenty to three. The quarterbacks that day were Bridgewater and Kaepernick—how time flies. But I understand why I needed to rest up after that one!

On September 22, 2015, I resumed my chemotherapy. I was so glad to have that extra week before I began this second round. My blood work right before my chemo revealed everything in the normal range. I hadn't had such good readings since before treatment began. As I had been told, this next round of chemo wasn't supposed to be so hard on my body. We were on track to finish my chemo in December, with surgery to follow a few weeks later. I thanked God for getting me this far, for always holding my hand and giving me an army of supporters. The Bible verse that gave me strength at this point in my journey was Isaiah 41:10. It reads, "So do not fear, for I am with you; do not be dismayed, for I am your God. I will strengthen you and help you; I will uphold you with my righteous right hand."

Move forward to October. I have just completed my third round of this second phase of chemo. My white count was holding, but my red count had dropped. Because of that, I was anemic and had trouble with fatigue. But compared to the first phase, this was easier to handle. I was incredibly humbled because that next weekend, my best friends Jaqui and Chy, and many others planned a benefit for me. My daughter and her fiancé had flown in from Phoenix, and all my family came. I was so grateful that Jim was well enough to attend and be by my side. Also attending were nearly one hundred additional people, including dear friends, Wayne and Sandy, from high school, along with my team and co-workers from Cabela's who helped organize the benefit. In addition, our neighbors from Monticello, a great friend and former boss from my days in Spicer, and many more friends and family attended. These were the same people who had comprised the "comfy quilt" from Caring Bridge, and that day I got to hug them in person and say thank you. The outpouring of their love, along with their generosity, was overwhelming. I felt ill that day and even had to escape into the bathroom and sit alone for a little while. But I wouldn't have missed that day for the world. God had decided it wasn't my time to leave this earth yet. I remember wishing so hard that day that I could also hug Him. But I knew His arms were surrounding me in love through the arms of our family and friends.

By now, I had gotten quite inventive at wearing different head wraps to hide my baldness. This became a mission as each week passed. In the very beginning, after losing my hair, I was devastated. But in the grand scheme of things and realizing what was truly important—losing my hair didn't even make the list now. It was a price to pay, but my eyes were on the prize of getting cancer free. So, wearing a scarf became second nature and a trivial piece of my journey.

Four days later, I had round four of twelve of my second chemo regimen. My hemoglobin continued to drop each week, causing elevated anemia. This was closely monitored and indicated I may need an additional transfusion. With my surgery scheduled for later in December, these numbers need to rise to be able to handle the mastectomy. But I continued to take one day at a time and leave it in God's hands. He has brought Jim and me this far, so I held strong in my faith that things would work out. But regardless of the outcome ahead, I had peace knowing that God's will would be done and not mine. As far as the low red blood count…I believe this, too, shall pass.

I LIFT UP MY EYES

My dear godmother, Gerry, wrote in my Caring Bridge journal that I had moved to the TOP of their prayer list. What a blessing she was to me on my journey. She told me to remember and hold on to Psalm 121:1-8. The words were so appropriate and still are to this day. I hope it can bring you as much comfort as it brought me. It reads as follows:

"I lift my eyes to the hills—where does my help come from?

My help comes from the Lord, the Maker of heaven and earth.

He will not let your foot slip—he who watches over you will not slumber

Indeed, he who watches over Israel will neither slumber nor sleep.

The Lord watches over you—the Lord is your shade at your right hand;

The sun will not harm you by day, nor the moon by night.

The Lord will keep you from all harm—he will watch over your life;
The Lord will watch over your coming and going both now and forevermore."

Thankfully, I had completed chemo round five of twelve, and my hemoglobin had risen. It only went up by 0.1—but I gladly considered it a win. I was still in the anemic range, but this was the first time it hadn't continued to drop. I met with the surgeon, and we discussed all my options. I learned what the process looked like before surgery, during surgery, and what to expect afterward. I was anxious to move forward but needed to practice patience and get through chemo first. Fifteen weeks down and seven more to go. They scheduled an ultrasound for the following week to check on the status of the tumor. Jim and I prayed for good news.

Round six of the twelve was bringing me to my knees. I was warned the symptoms would increase as we progressed into phase two. But this last treatment was like none other I had ever experienced. The fatigue had gotten so bad it was difficult to even walk across the room. My bones and muscles ached until the pain was almost unbearable. The neuropathy in my hands and feet had caused numbness and burning. I began running a fever and still was experiencing this when I went in for round seven.

Considering my debilitating symptoms, my doctor canceled chemo that day because of its toll on my body. I was given an IV of fluids to help with my dehydration. But it didn't stop there, unfortunately. I had been having trouble with bloody discharge and clots from my nasal passages, another unfortunate side effect of the chemo. So much for this phase being easier than "red devil!" She prescribed an antibiotic and made me an appointment to see an Ear, Nose, and Throat specialist to ensure the nasal septum had not been perforated. God again whispered, "I've got this," because the news was good. There was no perforation, and I was given two different meds twice daily to help heal the rawness inside my nostrils. Chemo is most definitely toxic to our bodies, but it was the price I had to pay to have a chance at stopping this aggressive cancer.

My oncologist was scheduled to meet with my surgeon to discuss stopping chemo and moving right to surgery. At some point, one must look at what chemo is doing to the rest of the body and make a medical decision. I met again with my surgeon the following week, and he said they would decide how we move forward. I trusted God and my doctors that the right path would be chosen.

For the past five months, I have been so blessed in having my friends, Jaqui and Chy, and their overwhelming loyalty, accompany me each week for my chemo appointments. You do not want to go through it alone; they had unselfishly given so much of their time. Once again, I need to give thanks to all those who followed me from the beginning on Caring Bridge. I repeat this often, but I cannot describe how much they meant. Nearly all of them had followed Jim's journey the previous five years, and here they were again, supporting us both through my journey. My cancer was so hard on Jim as he watched me suffer. But he was also comforted by all the outpouring of love and prayers for us both.

My medical team decided that chemo should be stopped, and I would have surgery in about two weeks once my body had regained strength enough to handle the procedure. My doctor ordered a chest X-ray and more blood work because my low-grade fever hadn't subsided. Praise God; all the results came back with nothing suspicious. My latest tests showed nothing alarming regarding the fever, but it would be closely monitored up to my surgery date. The ultrasound had shown the tumor had shrunk a little more and was responding to chemotherapy. The official date was chosen for my double mastectomy and was scheduled for December 10, 2015. What happens after that will be determined by what they find during surgery. They will see if the cancer is still present and if it has spread to the lymph nodes. This will determine if I need to finish my rounds of chemotherapy which had been halted. I really, really wanted chemo to be over, but whatever happened, I knew with God's help, I would get through this.

Psalm 121:1-2 "I lift up my eyes to the hills—where does my help come from?

My help comes from the Lord, the maker of heaven and earth."

I REPEAT...BELIEVE

Today is surgery day—December 10, 2015. Jaqui and Chy were there with me beforehand, along with my brother, Larry. I remembered all those times when Jim was repeatedly facing his health challenges. Although he was scared and uncertain of the future, he kept his humor for 98 percent of the time. So, in honor of him, I needed to do the same. I remember what I told my friends as the nurses wheeled me down the hall for my mastectomy. I looked back at them and said, "Well, wish me luck! I'm going for my weight reduction surgery!" After three and a half hours, I was out of surgery and resting in recovery. The surgery was successful, and the sentinel lymph node was removed to see if the cancer had spread into the lymphatic system. Once again, God answered our prayers, and no cancer was found in the node. Hallelujah! Later I left recovery and was wheeled up into my room. I was still so groggy from the anesthesia. I don't remember this part at all, but Jaqui said I mumbled how blessed I was and how thankful for all the people in my corner. Even though I have no memory of that - it certainly was the truth. Sidenote: I thought I would lose at least ten pounds out of the deal. But sadly, I was mistaken. I must have overestimated their size because I only lost about four pounds! I know I had a lot of fluid but give me a break! I'm sticking with my story that the hospital scale was sadly broken and needed repair!

My Caring Bridge journal was again a lifeline for me. Nearly one hundred entries were waiting from friends and family, all showing their support and thanking God for bringing me through this challenging journey. Two days later, as I lay in the hospital bed eating burnt toast and Cream of Wheat, I again spoke of how blessed I was. I didn't know how I would feel about having body parts sliced off. But I realized that if that was the price to pay for being alive—not a problem. These things had tried to kill me, so good riddance! I remember feeling that, in a very strange way—my cancer was almost a blessing. No, I hadn't lost my mind, and it wasn't the drugs talking. I truly believed that it brought my friends and family together into my "comfy quilt," and they got to share in the power of the Lord. I hoped that I could be an inspiration to anyone else who was facing this journey and to never give up. We don't get to choose how our story ends, but if we don't believe—we are not giving ourselves a fighting chance. By believing, we show God we trust Him no matter the outcome. So, whatever you face— please don't give up and keep fighting. Jim and I haven't given up; we have made it this far by God's grace. Always believe!

I was discharged on December 15, and my days back home were all about healing. I was getting used to the drainage tubes hanging from each side of my chest. I had to record the cc's of fluid and empty the collection tubes regularly. This wasn't something that excited me, but necessary. Once the drains were no longer releasing fluid from my chest, I returned to my surgeon to have them removed. Oh, my goodness, I had no idea how long they were. When he pulled each of them out of my chest, it felt like a garden hose coming out of my body. But they had done their job and helped keep me from complications. I also met with a specialist for a series of exercises because of my lymph node removal. I needed to do these exercises daily to prevent lymphedema. The last thing I was interested in at this point of the game was any complications.

I also met with my oncologist later in the month, and she explained that although the original tumor was not present anymore, several tiny cancer cells had broken off and were seen in the post-surgery testing of the tissue. Unfortunately, there were no guarantees that they were only isolated to the breast. The decision was made to be proactive and complete the final six rounds of chemo. These had been postponed back in November when I had gotten so sick. But now we needed to go back and finish them as an insurance policy with treatment to begin the first week in January. It wasn't what I wanted to hear, but after everything I had been through—the last thing I wanted was to take a shortcut now. We agreed this would be our greatest chance at hopefully fully beating this cancer. My cousin, Barb, had written in my Caring Bridge, "Since your dad sold insurance, he would certainly want you to take this insurance policy!" She was right, and I knew that my heavenly family of Dad, Mom, Lee, and Amy had also played a part in my journey. They were, no doubt, also woven into my "comfy quilt" all along,

We celebrated Christmas this year quietly but with peace. I had been given the greatest gift of all—the gift of life. Nothing anyone could have bought me would have even come close. It was a time to reflect on God's gift to us—the birth of Baby Jesus in the manger so long ago. God had chosen both Jim and me to remain on this earth, and we were so thankful we could share this Christmas with our families. Always Believe!

I began my last six rounds the first week in January. My blood count levels dropped somewhat, but nothing to stop my treatments. I had forgotten how rotten chemo makes you feel, but it did not stay forgotten long. But as I said before, I had come this far, and now I could see the light at the end of the tunnel. After this first round, I could say that I could count on one hand how many treatments I had left! It felt so good to say that and know I was on the home stretch. Each week my faithful friends were there by my side for my treatment. The chemo knew how to kick my butt, but I was much stronger inside than I was at the beginning of this journey. Each hurdle brought me closer to God, and I became stronger with each hurdle. I BELIEVED that I was winning the battle with our Savior's healing and with my family and friends. My "comfy quilt" woven by God held me tight with love, prayers, and support, and I never felt alone.

On February 9, 2016, I received my last treatment! No more fingers to count and no more poison being pumped into my body. The day was a celebration to enjoy the new life that had so graciously been given to me. At the beginning of my journey, my dear friends and I went to the casino to share memories before my cancer treatment began. Now on this day, we had a reason for a new celebration and one much happier than the first! I had finally finished treatment and beaten the monster. So, after my infusion, we were off to the casino for an overnight getaway to laugh, eat, have fun, and be thankful. Always believe!

FUR AND FOUR LEGS

I did have to face the reality that the next two years ahead would be the most critical. This particular cancer was relentless, and I would face follow-ups with my oncologist every three months. I always looked forward to these appointments. During my journey, I had a whole team of medical personnel who monitored me every step of the way. Now I was on my own, and this scared me. What if I had a subtle symptom that I would miss? What if the last doses of chemo weren't enough to stop those small cancer cells that had broken away? So, these appointments comforted me that I didn't have to face these possibilities alone. Together we kept close tabs on my health, and with each appointment, my odds became better.

At my first three-month appointment, my oncologist ordered a PET scan to check for any signs of reoccurring cancer. The results were great, and I was cancer free. There were those two words again…cancer free. Even though I was told this after my surgery, your mind likes to play games. But here we were, and those words were such a comfort. I continued these three-month appointments during my first two years post-treatment.

Each one brought me a new level of peace and brought me closer to that critical two-year mark. In addition, my doctor put me on medication in pill form to give me an even better chance at preventing this monster from returning.

It was like Jim had his own angel protecting him throughout my cancer. His angel had taken over for me while I was fighting my battle. There were a few bumps, but nothing compared to what the past had thrown his way. His seizures had, for the most part, subsided, and we both were so grateful. By the summer of 2016, Jim could get around with his walker's aid and feel free. We enjoyed coffee every morning on the deck with Gunner and Barney, just chilling in the sunshine. One of the biggest things we take for granted is our health. You don't realize it until it is threatened. For Jim, he had spent years battling through health scares. For me, the fight was only a little less than a year—but we both were so grateful now to enjoy the sunshine together.

Together we faced devastating sadness in January 2017. This time it was not our health but our dearly beloved dog, Gunner. He was diagnosed with cancer, and it became too painful to watch him suffer. Jim and I drove to the veterinarian and said goodbye to our loyal friend. He was as much a part of our journey as we were. He was always there anxiously waiting for Jim to return home from his multiple hospital and physical rehab stays. Any of you reading my book who are dog owners know exactly what I am talking about. The empathy and loyalty that Gunner portrayed were like no other. As Jim and I kept our belief along our journey, Gunner did as well. He would be so excited to see us whenever we returned home from our hospital stays. Dogs are no different than humans in one aspect. They crave love, companionship, and security. A quote from Stanley

Coren is as follows, "The greatest fear dogs know is the fear that you will not come back when you go out the door without them." Gunner patiently awaited our return, and the reunion was always glorious. Sometimes the best medicine we have has fur and four legs. Therefore, it was a sorrowful time for Jim and me the day Gunner crossed the rainbow bridge. Once again, we had to dig down deep into our faith. We had to believe that Gunner was now in a much better place and could run free through the fields again, as he had done at our country home. RIP, Gunner—you truly were man's best friend.

Over the next two years, Jim faced some additional skin cancer cases, with two of his spots being melanoma. He required Mohs surgery for these, as they were more severe. This procedure examines skin cells under a microscope to ensure all the cancer has been removed. Over the years, his skin cancer was mainly on his arms, face, and forehead. He also had one large area on his chest measuring four by four inches. This area required multiple treatments to control his cancer. But these cancer episodes represented thankful chapters in Jim's journey where he was NOT facing heart issues and/or seizures. He kept going and was a trooper through it all. He could live life again, something that had been taken away from him over the past six years.

Unfortunately, a few months later, I kept the excitement in our lives going. Our day-to-day life had become somewhat normal, and we surely couldn't have that! I decided to have an appendicitis attack in May of 2017. I was admitted to the hospital and underwent an emergency appendectomy. Things went well, and I was released back home the following day. We had learned over the years not to take our health for granted, so I accepted this as just another challenge to beat, and so I did.

Fast forward to February of 2018, when I went for a two-year check-up for my cancer. I was declared cancer free, and my doctor felt as much relief as I was. This cancer had a high return rate in one to two years, so I was blessed to have made it this far. The first two-year hurdle had been accomplished. Now I just needed to keep going, stay healthy, and enjoy life with Jim while remembering our Gunner's great memories.

THE NEVER-ENDING ROLLER COASTER RIDE

O ur so-called normal life did not last long. Looking back, I feel the timing was all part of God's plan. We needed to get me to my second anniversary before throwing anything major at us again. I didn't have guarantees that I would be home free, but the prognosis looked better for no reoccurrence. With each battle over these passing years, we became stronger in our faith and were better equipped for what lies ahead. As I said, our new normal was *not for long.* Ten days after my two-year checkup, we again faced a new uphill battle.

On February 21, 2018, Jim was experiencing some pain in his side. It came on so quickly and rapidly got worse. I drove him to the ER, and it was discovered he needed an appendectomy. Because he was on blood thinners, surgery could not be performed for twenty-four hours to reduce the risks. He progressively got sicker, and surgery was scheduled for the next morning. Once they got inside, they realized that waiting had a considerable cost. Unfortunately, his appendix had ruptured, with a portion already dying off. All we could say at this point was, "Please, God—we hope you have this!" Over the next ten days after surgery, Jim's condition worsened. An abscess was discovered, and he was put on antibiotics. But in a few days, after a scan was performed, it revealed that the abscess had instead grown. In addition, a second abscess was seen on the opposite side of his abdomen. They inserted a drainage tube at each site to help release the collected infectious fluid. And so, here began the roller coaster ride.

Unfortunately, the drain tubes weren't handling the infection. Also, his potassium levels had gotten completely out of control, and he began having severe cognitive issues. They struggled to find the proper dosage of potassium to correct this issue. It seemed like it was either too much or too little. Potassium is an electrolyte and helps to carry electrical signals to cells in the body. It is critical to adequately supply nerve and muscle cells, particularly heart muscle cells. Also, when potassium levels are too low, your kidneys retain more sodium, increasing blood pressure. This was all a recipe for disaster and was causing a huge metabolic issue. Jim began hallucinating and was having seizure-like movements and increased blood pressure. He talked randomly about things from his past and saw people in his room who weren't there. He also tried desperately to remove his drain tubes which would not have been a good move. They had to put giant mittens on Jim's hands so he couldn't pull on the tubes or remove his IVs. This was not the Jim we all knew and loved, and I prayed he could return to us. We hoped with all our might that "this too shall pass." But I'll be honest—the roller coaster ride needed to stop. I felt like vomiting in the fetal position and didn't know how much more we could take. As an earlier chapter referenced—I longed for the cheese curds and NOT the roller coaster ride. I knew I needed to once again turn this over to God. It was our only chance at getting off this sickening roller coaster ride.

As before, the prayers and support from Caring Bridge were there from all our friends and family. They had not missed a beat and were back as if time hadn't passed. Jim also had some visitors, but I had to prepare them for what they would see. Family and friends who visited included Jason, Byron, Amanda, Leo, Shayla, Carol, Maggie, Andrea, Natalie, Joshua, Jaqui, Chy and more. I knew it wasn't easy for them to see Jim drift in and out of reality. Everyone's hopes and prayers were for this not to be our last memory of him. I also prayed that Jim knew they were there and that he could feel their love.

The neurologist scheduled an EEG to detect electrical activity in the brain to see if that would give insight into the neurological symptoms. Typically, this is used to rule out epilepsy or brain tumors, among other things. It was now day twelve of his hospital stay, and he was scheduled for another cat scan to examine both abscess pockets. The left side looked good, but the right side not so much. They scheduled another surgery for that afternoon to replace the right-side tubing. That pocket remained very inflamed with infection, which explained his high white count of 17.3.

Day thirteen brought some much-needed good news. It was the first day in over a week that Jim was not having cognitive issues. He was "here" with us and not suffering from hallucinations. I prayed so hard that he didn't backslide and could keep this momentum going. The EEG results showed what they were thinking. It was a big name…acute encephalopathy. In normal words, it is a brain disease that alters regular activity. A combination of several things caused it. The contributors were appendicitis, high doses of antibiotics, kidney failure, and erratic potassium levels. The great news was that it wasn't permanent and could be treated with an adjustment of his IVs.

Jim's left abdominal drain was removed, and his right drain was flushed, and he would go for another scan in the morning. On day fourteen, he was still hallucination free, and his white count had dropped to 15.7. This level wasn't what they hoped for, but it was going in the right direction. But unfortunately, his scan revealed that one of his staples to the intestines from his appendectomy had let go. He was experiencing some leakage into the intestines, which must be closely monitored. But on this day, something was bringing me great joy. Jim began to joke with the nurses; everyone knew this was a great sign. And for the first time in two weeks, he could walk into the bathroom with a walker and one nurse assisting. To many, that's no big deal— so what if he walked a dozen steps? But to Jim, it was a huge deal. Just two days earlier, they were moving him with a motorized sling!

ENOUGH ALREADY

We were so grateful for every one of Jim's wins on this journey. My humble advice to anyone reading this book is to never take your health for granted. But every day, give thanks for what we take for granted. Philippians 4:4 reads, "Rejoice in the Lord always. Again, I will say rejoice!" Human nature makes it challenging to find joy in daily life. We love to focus on how unfair life has been and forget to thank God for the blessings He provides. Both Jim and I would never have wished for this to happen. But we chose to be grateful that this latest challenge was not the time for Jim's life on earth to end. As had happened so many times in previous years, here we were again and had much to be thankful for. We still held each other and shared our lives with friends and family. God was not done with Jim yet. Please teach yourselves to look for God when life throws you a curve ball. God's presence is always there, but he waits patiently for us to find Him. It is then that miracles can happen.

Day fifteen brought Jim closer to being discharged from the hospital. It was decided that he would go to a physical rehab facility to regain strength. His white count continued to drop and now read 14.1. He still had his right-side drainage tube and continued antibiotics. Day sixteen brought another drop in his white count—now at 12.7. The game plan was to have another blood draw in the morning, and if everything looked good —he would be moving to the physical rehab center. It will take a few weeks for him to regain his strength, but we are so relieved not to be back where we were just two weeks ago. Day seventeen and Jim was moving to the rehab center. I was apprehensive due to the fact his white count rose overnight. It was 13.6 and not the direction we wanted. But the nursing staff at the center will monitor this and keep an eye on his right drainage tube. He returned to Mercy Hospital days later for an appointment to do a follow-up scan to evaluate his right-side drain.

Jim's physical and occupational therapy went very well. Since he still had the drainage tube, he returned to the hospital on March 22 for a blood draw and scan to recheck the tube. His white count had now returned to normal at 6.3! Hallelujah! But with the good news came some bad news. They wanted to take another look at the surgery site to see the progress of his colon. As I mentioned, he had a complication with his incision staples at the junction of the colon. Today's scan revealed the colon was still leaking into the abscess area. Because of this, he could not have his tube removed, and we weren't allowed to get off the roller coaster. They decided to give him three more weeks, and if it hadn't healed by then—it meant going back into surgery to repair this area. Jim and I decided to "Believe," and we prayed he would not need additional surgery. That would be a challenge for him now; his body had been through enough. But through it all, Jim remained a big hit with the nurses and doctors. He would joke with them and, as was the custom, appreciated all the care they provided.

We were so hoping he could be home in time for Easter. But we received an even greater gift. Jim was released to go home on Palm Sunday, March 25, thirty-two days after his initial hospital admittance. They had arranged for in-home nursing to come and handle the drain tube, check vitals, and do blood draws. This was such a relief but also scary. He had been receiving round-the-clock care, and now it would be left in our hands, along with a nurse every two days. They trained me to care for his drainage tube between her visits. Again, just more experience for me in becoming a doctor! By now, I had to be getting closer to my medical degree, or so I thought. And just as excited as we were for Easter, we were so happy that this roller coaster ride had finally ended.

Sadly, after being home for two weeks, Jim was admitted to the hospital again, but this time for his heart. Jim had gotten off the roller coaster for fourteen days but now had boarded the ride again! Enough already—okay? After weighing in on the matter, Mercy Hospital spoke with Abbott Heart Hospital, and the decision was made to transfer him that same day. He was suffering from severe chest pressure and experiencing difficulty breathing. The transplant team had not provided his care during his appendectomy but had been consulted along the way. Their biggest concern was that Jim's body could reject his heart. His anti-rejection drugs had been cut in half to assist with his prolonged healing from his appendectomy. This gave his immune system a fighting chance at beating the infection. Rejection would be rare eight years after his transplant, but they could not afford to take that chance.

Thankfully all his testing looked good, and rejection was ruled out. We still didn't know if the hole in his intestine had healed, so we didn't know if surgery was still on the table (no pun intended). But his discomfort had passed, and after a day, he was again released to go home. He had multiple follow-up appointments over the next ten days leading to the colon scan. If it hadn't healed, he would need to have a section of his colon removed, which would be another battle for him to handle. We prayed, along with our "comfy quilt" of friends and family, and God whispered, "I've got this." On April 19, the scan revealed that the colon had healed itself. Praise God from whom all blessings flow. I was completely convinced that divine intervention had just taken place. With each week, it kept looking like surgery would be necessary. Then just like that —the colon was healed. And we FINALLY got off the roller coaster...again.

Almost Made It

Over the years, Jim would have some periods where he would be symptom-free. Sometimes these stretches were brief, but we cherished each and every one. It gave us a chance to have a somewhat normal life where Jim could get out and enjoy everything taken from him. It wasn't anything fancy—most weeks, it was a simple Thursday date night to Green Mill for a burger and play the meat raffle. These outings were a big deal to us, as it had been so many years when we couldn't even think of doing this. Jim was walking around the block with his walker every morning. To watch him on his walk was incredible. His walker was equipped with a seat so he could rest halfway. Most days, he would take Barney with him on the leash, and they would stroll the neighborhood together. It brought Jim so much enjoyment as he made his way back home.

Again, it was a simple thing to most, but it was an incredible feeling of independence and freedom to Jim. The curly long-haired Harley rider had this taken away from him so long ago. He had been unable to ride his bike for nearly fourteen years due to his declining health. Here was a man who lived and breathed

Harley and loved the independence of enjoying the sights and sounds of riding the highways. Now with everything he had faced over the years, a walk around the block was a huge deal. He was grateful for the ability to accomplish this—something that you and I sadly take for granted every single day.

Over the next year, Jim continued his walks around the block, coffee on the deck, and weekly dates to Green Mill for a burger and beer. Looking back, this year was one of the best regarding his health. It seemed as if we had finally settled into our new normal, and we were so thankful for each day we had together. Jim could spend time with our families and friends, and the memories we made were priceless. He was fortunate to be able to attend a few of Hunter's football games as well. This was my grandson, and Jim so loved being able to attend and cheer him along. One more thing brought "normalcy" back into our life. A bonus was my daughter and husband had moved from Arizona to Minnesota to be nearer family. This was a great gift that both Jim and I cherished.

In May of 2019, one of Jim's family generously gave us the gift of a cruise. Shannon and Carl accompanied us, and we left on Mother's Day for Mobile, Alabama, where we were to board the cruise liner. I had cleared the trip with Jim's doctors and took every precaution I could to meet any challenges we may have along the way. We had gotten our passports. I had several copies of his medication list, which totaled twenty-four different meds. I had a printout of his summarized health history, and I had put together twelve days of pills for him. The trip was Sunday through Saturday, but I always plan for the unexpected. Hey, wouldn't you, too, after what we had been through?

On Monday, we departed and began our adventure. I had scheduled a wheelchair at the docks for Jim because I knew he couldn't walk the distance to board the ship. Once on board, I arranged for a motorized scooter so he could easily get around the ship. We settled into our cabin and then went exploring. Neither of us had ever been on a cruise, and we were amazed at how large the ship was and all it had to offer. We spent the next four days enjoying ourselves with Jim's family members. We enjoyed the two stops in Mexico, and Jim could take his scooter off the ship and enjoyed the beach and shops. The one thing I learned quickly about a cruise is that you will never go hungry. The food was terrific, and it was everywhere. We enjoyed ourselves and were thankful for this opportunity to escape like ordinary people. It was so rewarding watching Jim being able to experience this cruise and get some of his life back again.

One particular memory from the cruise was Thursday when an honor service was held for veterans of all military branches. As each division was honored, they asked anyone in the audience to stand who had served. When they came to the ceremony for the army, I will never forget when Jim got up off his scooter and stood for the American flag and the US Army. He had tears in his eyes, and to witness the other cruise travelers who had also served was such an emotional moment. The cruise director led the ceremony and did a fantastic job honoring the veterans. At the time, little did I know the cruise director and the veterans would cross our path again.

It was now Friday, our last day at sea. We had gone up for the noon buffet earlier but decided to return later and visit the dessert bar. After thoroughly enjoying our desserts (yes, plural), we returned to our cabin to rest. Jim had been having trouble with fluid retention in his legs and feet for the past two days, so we would rest and elevate his legs in his bed to help control the swelling. As we each lay in our bed resting, I noticed him getting restless. And then the unthinkable happened. Jim had gone over two years without seizure activity, and we thought we had beaten that monster. But at approximately 3:00 p.m. on Friday, Jim began having a terrible seizure. I picked up the cabin phone, called down to the infirmary, told them what was happening, and requested they send a wheelchair asap to our room. I knew he couldn't ride his scooter in this condition and would need to be transported.

All I could think was how close we had come to having a perfect ending to our cruise. We had experienced a wonderful cruise together and were only eighteen hours away from the mainland when Jim's seizures began that afternoon. We were so close to reaching Mobile, Alabama, and deboarding the ship to fly home to Minnesota. We almost made it.

WE'RE SO SORRY...AGAIN

His seizures continued all the while walking through the narrow hallways towards the infirmary. We had to ensure he didn't fall out of the wheelchair, and I remember feeling so helpless. We made our way down and got him checked in with the nurse. The doctor came to see him, and Jim continued experiencing seizures. I returned to our cabin and got all the paperwork for his medical history and lengthy med sheet. They administered some medication to try and stop the seizures but with no success. The doctor asked if he could call back to the US mainland to consult with a neurologist. Jim laid there and held my hand with such sadness in his eyes that it broke my heart. He had been so excited to experience this cruise with no issues, and now that was all taken away. By now, the seizure activity was nearly continual, and Jim's blood pressure was spiking. The cruise doctor called the neurologist once again, and he instructed him that the only way to prevent Jim's heart from stopping was to intubate.

So here we were in the middle of the ocean with a cruise doctor who typically treated sunburn and sprained ankles. But now, he was asked to perform an intubation while at sea. The doctor performed the procedure, and Jim, at this point, was heavily sedated. They had to administer sedation meds at every fifteen-minute interval to control the seizing. The outlook would be grim if Jim remained at sea until we reached Alabama at 9:00 a.m. the following morning. Therefore, the decision was made to contact the Coast Guard for a sea evacuation. The cruise was not equipped with a ventilator machine, so a nurse was required to sit at his bedside and compress the airbag to provide the oxygen needed for Jim to breathe. Due to this, it was deemed impossible for Jim to be lifted in a basket up to a Coast Guard helicopter. That evacuation process takes two minutes to complete. Because there was no room for two people in the basket together, this would mean that Jim would be without oxygen for those two minutes. Therefore, a call went out to a Coast Guard cutter to have them transport Jim back to the mainland.

Time was not on our side as we waited for the cutter to arrive. I had given the medical team all of Jim's paperwork, including a copy of his passport. Jim also had his medical ID necklace that stated he was a heart transplant patient with the name of the hospital, that he was on blood thinners, a diabetic, and had non-epileptic seizures. Strangers would be transporting Jim in the middle of the night across the Atlantic Ocean headed for Mobile, Alabama. I needed to give them everything I could to prepare the medical team on the other end.

By now, it was approximately 1 a.m., and a cutter had been located and was on its way. So, this began the process of slowing down the cruise ship until it came to a stop. Unfortunately, it isn't as easy as stopping a car. This was much more complicated and time-consuming. But the cruise stopped just as the cutter was about one hundred yards away. Jim was carried by six crew members towards the bottom hatch of the ship, where the Coast Guard would load him onto the cutter. As we stood waiting, the ship captain received word that the cutter had a mechanical failure, and they could not steer the boat toward the ship. It felt like my heart was dropping right out of my body. It reminded me of when Jim was waiting for his transplant. We were informed a possible match was located, only to be told later, "We're so sorry." We were on such a critical timeline, and no one knew how much Jim's heart could handle the relentless seizures. Unfortunately, they had increased even more, and the medication was administered every five minutes.

We were again years later with "I'm so sorry," and I struggled with how our God could let this happen. I remember my faith thermometer diving, and all I could say was, "Why God?" It was clear Satan was at work once again. When we are at our lowest, he swoops in to shatter our faith and take us to a dark place. This is when we must cry to God to wrap us in his heavenly arms and keep our faith thermometer from plummeting downward.

Don't get me wrong...this is a challenging thing to do. Partnering with Satan is the easy way out; as humans, it is the path of least resistance. But it is always our best option to choose God over Satan every single time. He will provide us with the strength we need if we ask. But if we try to go it alone—sorry, we don't have a chance. But even though I chose God over Satan, I must be honest. I still asked why. It is natural to do so as humans, but I believe God understands. He doesn't want us to take up residency in our pity party. We need to brush it off and hold on for dear life.

Faced with the new circumstances, the cruise captain obtained permission from the Coast Guard to resume travel, but at a higher speed than allowed by law. So, after coming to a complete stop in the middle of the night, the ship began increasing speed to race back to Alabama. There were no guarantees whatsoever that Jim would survive this trip. Through what had happened so far, I was fortunate to have Jim's two family members there and a wonderful staff member from the cruise. It was overwhelming to process, and I had to pray for strength, but mostly to remain calm. In the past, every time Jim and I faced a new health scare—I always did my very best to remain calm for him. But this situation was like nothing we had experienced in the past. This time, we couldn't just call the ambulance and arrive at a hospital twenty minutes later. Therefore, with more divine intervention and my God-given "comfy quilt," I did my best to remain strong for Jim.

As we were returning to the US, I went to my cabin for about five minutes to get some Tylenol. While I was there, I received a call from the doctor. A second Coast Guard cutter had been located and was racing to the ship. I ran back to the infirmary, and once again, the ship slowed down and stopped. I remember thinking about all the other passengers on the ship and what could be running through their minds. First, it's the middle of the night, and we slow down and stop, then we speed up only to slow down and stop again. I hoped with all my heart that this wouldn't be another "I'm so sorry." But this Coast Guard cutter successfully reached the ship, and the six crew members returned once again to carry Jim towards the hatch and the waiting boat.

COUNT YOUR BLESSINGS

Jim was unconscious, and I was so afraid as they carried him through a short and narrow hallway to the waiting Coast Guard. It was now 3:00 a.m., and as the hatch opened, I could see the huge waves of the ocean in the cutter's lights. I felt numb as I watched Jim lowered into a narrow "sled" where he would be guided down to the cutter. Two nurses went with Jim—one to operate the airbag and a second to administer his seizure meds at five-minute intervals. I wanted to go with Jim badly but was not granted permission due to space restrictions. The cutter already had its' own personnel on board, and Jim and the two nurses. I stood there as the hatch was closed and prayed to God that Jim's body could handle this dangerous trip across the ocean in the darkness of night.

As I think back to that night, looking out the open door from the belly of the cruise liner—I remember so vividly seeing the huge waves of the ocean and the rocking back and forth of the Coast Guard cutter. It was total darkness except for the boat's lights. Today this reminds me of the passage in Matthew 8 where Jesus calmed the sea. In verses 23-24, it reads: "Then he got into the boat, and his disciples followed him. A furious storm came up on the lake without warning, so the waves swept over the boat. But Jesus was sleeping."

Let me stop there. The disciples were tossed around on the boat amid a terrible storm. They were so afraid and feared for their lives. And what was Jesus doing? He was sleeping. Before He ever stepped onto that boat, he knew the outcome and remained calm enough to sleep. But the disciples were freaking out and had lost their faith. In Matthew 8:25-27, we read, "The disciples went and woke him saying, Lord, save us! We're going to drown! He replied, You of little faith, why are you so afraid? Then he got up and rebuked the winds and the waves and it was completely calm. The men were amazed and asked, What kind of man is this? Even the winds and the waves obey him!"

Jim would be facing the high seas just as the disciples did. It is human nature to be afraid—that is how we are wired. But we need to cut the wires on our fear and put our trust in God. As I mentioned in an earlier chapter...If you are going to worry, don't bother praying. In today's world, we hear the phrase "cancel culture." Well, this is cancel culture at its finest. Worry cancels prayer. It causes us to second guess ourselves, and we want to throw in the towel. Fear is a debilitating emotion that clearly causes our faith thermometer to nosedive. But just as Jesus calmed the storm for His disciples—He will calm our storm. It may not be in the timeline we wish, but He will bring calm when it is His time. Our only assignment during the storm is to turn to God, pray for strength, and rest in the fact that His loving and protective arms surround us.

As I have learned so clearly over the years, every storm has trials and blessings. We must thank God for what is good and right in the situation. We then pray for His help for what is not good and right in the storm. I needed to focus on what our blessings were at that moment. The cruise doctor was able to intubate Jim successfully. Jim was still alive. A second Coast Guard cutter had been located. The cruise personnel were outstanding in assisting us through this unbelievable turn of events. Two nurses were available to accompany Jim providing the medical attention necessary to give him a fighting chance at survival. There were so many blessings to be grateful for. This is a great life lesson, and we must do our very best to practice this every *time* we are faced with a storm. Count your blessings, and then, and only then, turn the rest over to God.

What happened next, I will never forget as long as I live. I went back to our cabin and put on the television. They had a channel where a camera from the front of the ship gave you a view of the sea ahead. I could see the Coast Guard lights racing across the ocean in front of our ship towards the mainland. Soon, the cutter was out of view, and I only saw total darkness. I felt this darkness inside my soul as I stood there helpless. Somehow, I knew I had to keep my composure and wait anxiously until morning when we reached the mainland. I knew I couldn't sleep, so I packed our belongings. As I'm sure all tourists do, we bought souvenirs at the two stops in Mexico. I couldn't fit everything into the suitcases, so I left in the room some things brought from home that our souvenirs had now replaced.

Jim's family and I went down to the main area for deboarding and began our wait. While waiting for approval to get off the ship, one of the staff members told me I had forgotten several things back in my cabin. This was everything I had decided to leave behind so I could take our souvenirs home. They had put everything into a large garbage bag and brought it to an office nearby. I walked in there and saw everything I had purposely not packed. I knew I was already going to have to handle our luggage and couldn't possibly carry a large garbage bag as well. I thanked them but told them to help themselves to whatever was inside and returned to our waiting area. At this point, my concern was not with the contents of the garbage bag.

While sitting there with our suitcases, I suddenly noticed the cruise director walk by. He and the veterans had touched Jim's heart so much during the military ceremony. I approached him, and what I did next was only possible through a God-given strength. It was as if God Himself told me I needed to do this. With all my might, I hoped that God was again whispering, "I've got this." I informed the director what had happened over the past eighteen hours. I asked him if he would consider asking any veterans who felt it in their hearts to say a prayer for Jim. He immediately agreed, hugged me, and we said a brief prayer together. Then shortly, an announcement came over the ship's intercom letting the military vets know that one of their own needed their support. He asked any vets willing to please say a prayer for Jim. It was an emotional moment, and I could feel their support and many other passengers not in the military. In such a dark time, it was a ray of light and a sign of hope that I needed to sustain myself for what was next.

SO, IS THERE ANYTHING WE NEED TO KNOW?

O nce all the customs requirements were met, we could leave the ship. The cruise personnel had received word from customs about which hospital Jim was transported to in the early morning. As we pulled our multiple suitcases along, we went to transportation, where the taxis and buses were located. Jim and I each had a suitcase and a carry-on, so as the first cab came into sight, I was allowed to take it and proceed to the hospital. I remember thinking I was in a strange city and far from home. I had absolutely no idea as to the status of Jim's health. I had to face the reality that I might be too late in getting to him. Had he survived the trip to shore? Did the hospital receive his medical information and know his complicated history? Had the seizures subsided? Was he conscious? Had his heart kept beating throughout all the seizures? I couldn't stop my brain from spiraling and I needed to get to that hospital.

As the cab driver pulled up to the curb, he unloaded all four bags of my luggage, got in his car, and drove away. I walked with all the luggage through the hospital entrance and to the front desk. I felt numb as I asked the person working for Jim's room number. I gave him his full name and birthdate. He replied, "Sorry, we don't have anyone here by that name." I asked him to check again, and his reply was the same. I stood there, not having a clue what to do next. Had customs given the cruise the wrong information regarding the hospital? Then an overwhelming cold sweat came over my body, and I thought, what if I was too late and Jim had passed? I stood there motionless, and the front desk employee could see how fragile I was. He replied, "We do have a John Doe up in ICU if you want to check that out?"

I gathered my luggage, proceeded to the elevator, and went up to the ICU floor of the hospital. I asked the nurse which room John Doe was in, and it took every ounce of my courage to walk down that hall to the room number she provided me. As I turned the corner and walked into the room, I prayed that it please be Jim. At this point, it would tell me he was still alive. I entered and looked at the bed. I saw a patient with almost their entire head wrapped and multiple wires attached. These led to a large machine next to the bedside. But I could see some of the patient's face, and it was Jim! I have written the words for my book thus far, but at this moment, I cannot find the words to explain how I felt. I was scared and alone, but I was relieved that I wasn't too late and Jim still had a fighting chance at survival.

The nurse came in and asked if I knew this patient. I explained to her what had happened over the last twenty hours. I asked her where his medical information, passport, med list, and med alert necklace were. She explained that he came in with nothing except the shirt on his back. I was angry because I had been so prepared and brought all this information to the cruise infirmary to hand over to the Coast Guard. Unfortunately, I will never know who dropped the ball. But what mattered most now was they were unaware a patient in their hospital had a heart transplant, was diabetic, had a history of seizures, and was on blood thinners. They were treating him blindly for seizures without knowing anything else. She instructed me to go to admissions to get him checked in and submit his insurance information. I get it; they needed his insurance info, but that wasn't my priority. I asked if I could leave my luggage there while I went to admissions. She replied no because it wouldn't be safe, and they couldn't be held responsible. So, I returned to the elevator with four suitcases full of dirty laundry and went to admissions.

After about twenty minutes, I gathered my luggage and returned to the ICU to Jim's room. The nurse summoned a doctor to let them know the patient had been identified. He walked in, and I will never forget the words that came out of his mouth," So tell me, is there anything we need to know about this man's health history?" Are you kidding me? I told him to take a seat, and then I proceeded to bring him up to speed. I also gave him a copy of all the paperwork they had never received earlier. As soon as they learned of the complexity of Jim's health, some drastic changes were made. They ordered anti-rejection drugs for his heart transplant. In addition, they checked his blood sugar and administered insulin. They took him off epilepsy medication once they knew these were not epileptic seizures. It was all so surreal. I almost felt like I was having a nightmare and would wake up soon. How could this have happened in a US hospital?

But there wasn't time to think about that now. They had sedated Jim so heavily, and he was on a respirator. Now I had to anxiously wait for him to wake up. I sat there alone and helpless, watching his every breath. Finally, after about three hours, he woke, and I could look into his warm eyes again for comfort. He could not speak because of the respirator, but they removed the breathing tube two hours later. He could breathe on his own, and it was such a relief to the medical team and me. He was not very coherent, but this was expected for everything he had been through. He had been given massive doses of anti-seizure meds for nearly twenty hours, and his body had to fight back.

The testing performed with the electrodes on his brain showed no concerns. Praise God! But we knew we weren't out of the woods yet. Later in the afternoon, he developed a fever, and his white count rose to twenty. They began several blood cultures to try and identify the problem. In addition, his blood pressure was significantly elevated from not having any of his heart meds. They began those, and for the remainder of the day, he rested and lay there helplessly as they continued drawing blood and checking vitals. A big challenge for me was the ICU visiting hours. They refused to budge on them, and I had to go to a tiny waiting room from time to time throughout the day and early evening.

God stepped in once again and threw me a lifeline. He brought to me in person a member of my "comfy quilt." Jim's son, Bryon, lived in Minnesota but worked out of state in Oklahoma. His boss graciously rented a car for him, and Byron drove several hours and arrived at Mobile late that night. Having him there in a strange city far away from home was comforting. Because Jim had experienced three more seizures around 9:00 p.m., we were permitted to stay in his room. They sedated him once again to help him sleep through the night. Byron and I each sat on a very hard folding chair they provided, and this is where we spent the night. I remember it was chilly in the room, and I had to take some dirty clothes out of my suitcase and layer them to keep warm. The nurses were in every hour throughout the night to check his vitals and to give him short neurological tests.

Unfortunately, at 5:00 a.m., Jim experienced two additional seizures and, therefore, more sedation. Byron and I sat there so helpless; the agony of watching Jim go through this was almost too much to bear. Superman was struggling again for his life and finding anything "super" about the situation was difficult. After such a long time of being seizure-free—they had reappeared out of nowhere and were threatening the survival of Jim's heart and his life.

After two days of multiple tests, blood draws, specialists, and scans—Jim was finally given the okay to be transferred from ICU to another room. This made all of us very happy. Jim didn't have to be under ICU supervision anymore. Byron and I had comfortable chairs and much more room to store our luggage without the nurses tripping over them. The seizures had now subsided, and his blood pressure was better regulated - so that meant only one thing. Jim had begun his joking and teasing with the hospital staff. They were unaware of this side of Jim, so it took them a while to realize what he was up to. But soon, he was in his old rhythm, and they would hand it back to him with ease and a smile. This was a good sign that the "old Jim" was coming back to us.

Later that day, he experienced some heart rhythm irregularities. Bloodwork revealed his potassium had tanked, and they believed this was the cause. They promptly administered doses to help raise his levels. They were correct, as his heart rate had once again improved. Now, with every staff member that entered his room, he had one question for them. "Can I go home now?" We were gradually getting closer to making that happen, and we thanked God and our army of prayer warriors for bringing us the strength to get through this near-death experience. Once again, let me repeat. Psalm 32:7, "You are my hiding place; you will protect me from trouble and surround me with songs of deliverance."

DO YOU WANT ME TO DRIVE?

I had been partnering with Jim's transplant team in Minnesota during our stay in Mobile. With hours of coordination between doctors, nurses, and social workers in Mobile and back home—we were getting closer to his discharge. We had to cancel our original flight home from the cruise for apparent reasons. Given our circumstances, everyone agreed Jim should not fly in case of unexpected health issues. By now, we were accustomed to "unexpected health issues" and agreed to drive to Minnesota.

The following day we were waiting for the final okay from the medical team. Jim had fallen asleep when we received a pleasant surprise. His brother Bob, and his wife, Angie, had driven four hours to visit Jim in the hospital. We had approximately forty-five minutes with them when the doctor came in and said those magic words, "You can go home now." Byron, Bob, Angie, and myself gathered everything and wheeled Jim downstairs to our rental car that Byron had reserved for our return trip. All the rental company had available was a small compact car, but we were determined. We packed all our luggage in there, and I squeezed into the back seat with just enough room to breathe. At this point, I would have been happy to be strapped up on the roof of the car to get back home. Jim and Bryon were in the front seat, and we were ready for our twenty-hour drive back to Minnesota.

Because I had brought extra days of medications for Jim on our cruise, I still had enough to get us back home. The hospital had added two new prescriptions, and we stopped at a local drug store and picked those up along with car chargers and snacks. We were so grateful for the care Jim received on the cruise and again at the hospital. Although there were some bumps along the way, the bottom line was that Jim's life had been saved, and that was all that mattered. We also had our "comfy quilt" of Caring Bridge followers who once again were with us in prayer on this latest journey. Our blessings continued to amaze us, and we again thanked God that Jim was allowed to return to his Minnesota home rather than make the final journey to his heavenly home.

Since we didn't leave Mobile until midafternoon, we only drove five hours that first day. We quickly stopped at Walmart to pick up a walker for Jim and some pillows. We made it to Jackson, Mississippi, and checked into a hotel. Jim was not strong enough to walk to the elevator and down the hall to our room. The desk clerk graciously let us take a rolling office chair, and we pushed Jim from the entrance to the elevator and up to our room. Byron took a handful of our dirty clothes along with his laundry and washed them in the hotel laundromat. I was able to take a shower—the first in six days! I, and everyone around me, learned very quickly that deodorant only goes so far!

After a good night's rest, we ventured out again, heading towards Minnesota. We had to stop often so Jim could stand alongside the car and stretch his legs. He needed to keep them elevated to help prevent fluid buildup. At the beginning of the trip, we tried having him sit in the back with his legs across the seat. His 6'2" stature wasn't a great fit for the back seat of our compact car. Since this wasn't working well, he moved up front and put his legs under a pillow on the dash. At this point, his memory of what had just happened was somewhat foggy. In his mind, he was good to go, and repeatedly would ask Byron if he wanted him to drive. Every time he would ask, Byron would look in the rearview mirror at me and smile. He always replied, "No, thank you—I've got this, Dad." I think possibly that even God was whispering, "No, Jim…I've got this! You leave the driving to us!"

The second day brought a few challenges. It was tornado season, and we had to dodge some nasty storms. We decided to stop after eight hours of driving rather than risk driving right into the storms. We spent the night in Hannibal, Missouri, only miles from the Iowa border. A severe thunderstorm happened overnight, but our prayers for safe travel have been answered. After going to bed early and getting up early, we took off for the final leg of our trip home. Jim had been very sleepy the past two days from one of the new anti-seizure meds and wanted nothing more than to get home to his living room recliner. We all had sore backs, were so tired, and more than anything, wanted to get home. We couldn't have predicted or prepared for the past nine days. Who gets rescued by the Coast Guard at high sea to lie in a strange and faraway hospital as John Doe?

Around 3:00 p.m. on the third day, we rolled into Blaine and reached our Home Sweet Home. After getting Jim settled, I drove Byron about an hour away to his car, and he drove back home to Spicer, and I returned to Blaine. We knew that God had once again whispered, "I've got this." By now, we couldn't even begin to count how many times God had whispered this to us, but we kept giving Him our sincere thanks each and every time. The Bible says that with each trial we face, God walks beside us and deepens our strength. Well...let's say Jim and I were getting pretty strong!

The following day, Jim's doctor visited the home to see him. We were so fortunate to be in a program where his doctor, nurse, therapist, and more all came to Jim rather than him having to get to the clinic. We were approached about this new program after Jim had suffered his ruptured appendix. It was a relief for Jim and me not to have to travel to see his doctor. We didn't know this existed but were thankful they asked us to participate. The doctor ordered a complete blood panel, and the health team came to the house at 5:00 p.m. for the blood draw. Later that same day, at 7:45 p.m., a mobile unit came to the house for an EKG and a chest X-ray. I can't say we have ever had an X-ray machine in our living room! But we both felt having these excellent medical services was impressive, especially late on a Friday before Memorial weekend.

Jim's bloodwork came back good for all results except one. His potassium was back up to normal, his white count was back down to normal, but his kidney functions were showing distress. Given all he had been through the past nine days, they still hoped these levels would return to normal. Slowly Jim was getting a little strength back and was walking short distances with his walker in the house. He tired quickly but needed to keep circulation moving to prevent blood clots.

His doctor was scheduled to return on Tuesday to review the X-ray and EKG and to help set up an appointment with a neurologist. We also needed to schedule an appointment with his dermatologist as a few suspicious skin spots had appeared on his arm. But we were taking one day at a time and remained holding tight to our anchor—our faith.

TAKE NOTHING FOR GRANTED

After being back home for three days, our world came crashing down. On Memorial Day, Jim again began having seizures and was taken by ambulance to Abbott. I tried so hard not to be angry with God, but Satan was again shouting in my ear to be angry—be very angry! I just wanted to ask why this was happening all over again. But instead, I needed to focus on our blessings. Jim's life had been saved in Alabama. We had safely driven back home to Minnesota without any seizures. We were back in the Allina health system, where everyone knew Jim's medical history. So, as I drove to the hospital—I kept repeating these blessings and told Satan just to shut up.

Jim was admitted to the stroke unit at Abbott and given an MRI. In addition, they placed electrodes on his head, as they had done in Alabama. This would track all brain activity if and when he had another seizure. Jim's transplant team was only two floors down and would visit in the morning. So, we began a waiting game for answers.

Jim suffered one seizure at 8:00 p.m. that night, giving the medical team essential data from his brain activity. He remained "wired" for monitoring, and they continued to review his brain waves. We desperately prayed for answers and, more importantly, a game plan on what's next. Jim's body couldn't continue handling this number of seizures without grave consequences. The following morning was a rough one for Jim. He suffered eight more seizures from 8:00 a.m. to 10:00 a.m. With all that activity, they could read the brain waves and fully confirm that these were non-epileptic seizures. These types of seizures are not typically treated with medication but can be caused by infection or external factors.

They determined to stop his night-time seizure med administered on the cruise and in Mobile, as it was ineffective for non-epileptic seizures. They continued to monitor him and look for answers. That evening Jim did not experience any seizures overnight after halting the medication. He had gone twenty-four hours without a seizure, and no words could express our thankfulness. Each seizure Jim has suffered over the years took a huge toll on his body. They would exhaust him, and the uncertainty was so unsettling. On a lighter note—his first stress test was the prior evening when Jim couldn't watch the Minnesota Twins on his TV. The hospital had revamped the TVs that afternoon, and now the Fox Sports North channel was gone. Jim had to choose another channel and rely on the Twins to win without him. Go Twins!

Finally, two days later, the neurologist ordered the electrodes removed, and Jim could be rid of the monitor. They were completely satisfied that these were non-epileptic seizures and that the meds begun on the cruise and continued in Mobile should remain discontinued. Jim's episodes completely resemble a seizure but were not brain related. The medical team agreed on how Jim and I would handle these seizures going forward.

We were instructed to remain at home, and I would help to keep Jim calm. We would get through the episode together, and I would help ensure his safety. They assured us the seizures were non-medical and there would be no need to call 911. It was scary that we would be handling these ourselves in the future, but on the flip side, it would save Jim numerous ambulance rides and countless hours of waiting in the ER.

The following day after internal medicine, neurology, and cardiac all signed off—Jim was given the okay to return home again. This experience was an example of counting our blessings and never taking things for granted. I repeat myself, please do not take everyday experiences for granted. Walking to the mailbox, sitting on the deck drinking your morning coffee, having a phone conversation with a loved one, getting around your home without worrying about falling or seizures…they all happen without us giving them a second thought. But for Jim, these accomplishments had been sadly taken from him. He would give anything to experience them once again without a dark cloud of worry overhead. So please be grateful for all the little things in life. When you pray to God, don't forget to thank Him for all the everyday "stuff" that is so easy to take for granted.

Six days later, Jim had his semi-annual appointment with the transplant team. We arrived at 7:00 a.m. for labs followed by bloodwork, multiple tests, and scans. Since his discharge a week earlier, he had not experienced any seizures, but today would be a test. From leaving home early that morning until we returned later that evening—it was a twelve-hour day for Jim. He passed with flying colors and was glad to get back home again. Now we had one prayer to give God. We wished for a dull life. That's all we wanted at this point. No ambulances, hospitals, or seizures. Nothing but dull. We both agreed this would make us so very happy.

BUBBLE WRAP

Jim, aka Superman, faced a brand-new challenge months later. He was regularly experiencing massive amounts of bleeding from his mouth. He would wake up and be blood-soaked in bed, and we would rush to the ER to get it under control. Of course, being on blood thinning medication to prevent clots didn't help. After this happened several times, it was determined that his anti-rejection drugs had compromised much of the bone structure in his jaw, and infection had set in. We began a series of several appointments at the University to begin extracting Jim's teeth. Because he was such a high risk, they performed between four and six teeth at a time to ensure his heart wasn't under stress. The process lasted months, from beginning to end, and he was finally fitted with dentures.

In 2020 the world faced a pandemic that would alter everyone's life. Except for one person, and that was Jim. Because his health was frail and he would experience occasional seizures, it made it difficult for him to leave home. The lockdown didn't change his lifestyle, as he was already practicing this in real life. So, we pushed through the lockdown and the years to follow by doing all we could to keep our lives healthy and free from complications. It was challenging for Jim; as every day passed, he lost more and more of his freedom. He could only walk short distances in the house with his walker. He continued to suffer seizures, and this always brought fear. We couldn't risk any more falls, so we adapted. Going forward, I would follow him with the wheelchair while he used his walker to go twenty feet from his recliner to the bathroom.

On several occasions, he would suffer a seizure while in the bathroom. This made things even more difficult as the half bathroom was very small. The door was hard to open as Jim was just to the right behind the door. I would squeeze myself into the space and help prevent him from getting injured. Once the seizure had passed, I would help him into the wheelchair and take him back to his recliner. There were many days when he was unable to walk. We would then skip the walker, and I would take him to and from the bathroom in the wheelchair. This was difficult for Jim as he watched every ounce of his independence being robbed. I kept reassuring him that it was okay—I was here to help and wasn't going anywhere. We took one day at a time and left the future to God. But my heart silently broke for Jim as he faced this struggle daily. Miraculously, he still didn't take these opportunities to complain. He remained positive and hid any disappointments he may have had from me.

In the past, Jim had suffered bad falls on the three steps leading from the garage into the house. When he did fall, I would always go down with him by trying to stop his fall. I was not much of a match for his six foot two inches and two hundred and sixty-five-pound stature. I would wheel him in the wheelchair from the car and then sandwich it between us on the steps into the house. One fall we both went backwards down the three steps to the cement garage floor. We were both so worried about each other but were so fortunate only to suffer some bumps and bruises. I truly believed God was there and wrapped His arms around us to protect us. He was our *"bubble wrap"* and kept us safe.

But only to be explained by God's intervention, Jim would climb the stairs to the upper level of the house every evening and back down again every morning. There are no bedrooms on our main floor, and Jim chose to climb the stairs. This everyday challenge was his only exercise for the entire day, and he was unwilling to give up this last piece of his independence. It also provided a small amount of hope in keeping blood clots away. Our stairs have a landing halfway up, and I placed a chair there for Jim to stop and rest. I would sit on the stairs above him and talk while he rested. He would often have a seizure while sitting there, and I would calmly speak to him and ensure he didn't fall off the chair. Once the seizure had passed, I would follow him the rest of the way up the stairs. This was such a worry for me every single day, but it brought him such a feeling of accomplishment that I couldn't be the one to take it away. God's "bubble wrap" kept Jim safe as he daily maneuvered the stairs.

I was fortunate to have my son Jason here when I had to leave the house. I would run to get groceries and shop quickly to return home. With him here, it gave me a sense of security and eased the guilt of leaving Jim home to be alone. The seizures were always the enemy and could bring Jim the most significant physical harm. But this was the hand we were dealt; we always had two options. We could choose option one and complain and be miserable or accept, let go, and let God. Option two always was and always would be our only option. It is similar to when we get dumped on in Minnesota with a foot of snow. We can complain and be miserable, but we still have a foot of snow at the end of the day. And to top it off, we were miserable all day. So, this option doesn't accomplish anything except misery. The lesson here is *don't choose this option!* Give everything to the Lord and look for the positives in life. They are there, and it's a shame when we ignore or miss them altogether.

I BELIEVE IT'S TIME

We continued our life at home, doing everything possible to keep Jim safe. He was still experiencing seizures, and I would do whatever I could to prevent him from falling. At his semi-annual appointment for his transplant in December of 2021, it was discovered Jim's white count had skyrocketed once again. It had reached twenty-one and indicated something serious. The team wanted Jim to see an oncologist, but he refused. He told them he had beaten death so many times, but he was not up to the fight this time. He knew chemotherapy and radiation would be more than he could handle, so he decided to let this be. Superman was tired and knew that his time of superpowers was fading. Hearing him speak these words was difficult, but I respected his decision and understood completely. As he said, he was tired and didn't have the will to fight even once more. This was a sad day for us both, but we hid our feelings to spare the other.

Early one evening, only about a week later, Jim was experiencing severe chest pain and numbness down his arm. He had made clear to all his medical providers years ago that he did not want any life-saving measures and would face the music—whatever it may be. I gave Jim nitro to help ease the pain and held his hand. I asked him if he was sure he wanted to remain at home. He answered softly that he did and then indicated he wanted to call his family members. One by one, I dialed and held the phone to his ear, and he said his goodbyes. It was such an emotional time, but seeing the peace on his face was my strength. His pulse had slowed, and he was very pale as he sat quietly in his chair. I had called the transplant team earlier to let them know of his condition, and because of his wishes, they agreed to let him remain home.

But suddenly, it was as if God had entered the room and said, "Nope—not yet." Jim began feeling a little better, and the pain subsided. So, we sat quietly for about fifteen minutes, and like a miracle, Jim recovered from what I truly believe was a heart attack. For reasons only God knew, it wasn't Jim's time to leave this earth. It was a frightening moment, while strangely also filled with peace.

Two months later, we were on our nightly climbing the stairs to bed. He was sitting on the landing chair, and I was on the steps. We were talking as we did every night while he rested. He looked at me and said, *"I believe it's time."* I wasn't sure what was happening or what he meant by this. He said living at home had become too much of a challenge for him and me. I told him I was fine, but he insisted we begin looking into nursing homes for him. This had to be Jim's decision, as he had given up so much in the past, and I would never think of taking this one last shred of independence from him. I never expressed my fear to him, but I always thought, what if I would ever cause him severe injury by not being able to protect him by myself? It was something that I was so afraid of, but I didn't want to put that burden on him, so I never said it aloud. But now he had made the choice, and I needed to respect it and begin the next challenging step.

Jim expressed his wishes to return to where his children had grown up. He had worked there for many years in the school district. He also had served as a Boy Scout master for several years and had many friends still living there. On February 29, 2022, we made a visit with his son Byron to the nursing home in his hometown. Seeing how everything would change in Jim's world was difficult, but he again expressed that this was what he wanted. To this day, I'm not so sure he indeed did, but his generous and warm heart may have chosen this for others. I wrote about the last night Jim spent at our home in my journal. Here is my entry—"Dear Lord, this is Jim's last night in our home. We have had nearly eight years here in this house and have faced many health challenges. I pray for Jim at his new home and pray that You will protect him from harm and danger. I pray that his seizures will subside, and he can enjoy his time on earth. Thank you, God. Amen." After several phone calls, paperwork, and insurance changes—Jim entered the nursing home on Friday, March 11, 2022. Both of our worlds changed dramatically that day.

After being Jim's caregiver nonstop for the past twelve years—I struggled with the thought of not being there with him 24/7. It wasn't a reflection of the nursing home but my own feeling of guilt for not being his sole caregiver anymore. It was the world I knew, and I didn't know how to begin this new life now where others were responsible for his care, meds, and every need. I had prepared a complete summary for the staff of his medical past. To say his history was complicated would be the biggest understatement ever. I also wanted to give everyone a heads-up on his history of seizures. I needed to know they understood that medical attention was not required. As the doctors had instructed—they needed to sit with him to ensure his safety and not call 911. This would cause Jim more anxiety as the local hospital would want to begin brain scans and all the testing. Jim had been there and done that so many times before, and I didn't want him to have to suffer through it once again. I had prepared a document thoroughly describing his seizures and how to proceed when they occur. I requested that every staff member read this before spending time with Jim. It was for their benefit, as well as his.

The first two nights, I stayed at my son Travis's home, about twelve miles away. During the day, I would sit with Jim and be sure everything was going well for him in his new environment. On Sunday late afternoon, I made the trip back home to Blaine. Leaving him was hard, but we agreed to call each other often. I spoke with him twice on my drive back, and he called me again that evening before I went to bed.

Jim was in an isolation wing of the nursing home because he didn't have a covid booster. His room was two short hallways off the main hallway, and I worried because the staff were not nearby. In the previous twelve years, I was his caregiver, and now as I returned home, I was two hours away and wasn't there to be with him if he needed help. We said our good nights over the phone, and I slept. Very early in the morning, I received a call that, during the night, the staff had found Jim on the floor in his room. He had gotten up to go to the bathroom and suffered a seizure. He had fallen, hit his head, and lay there for quite some time. I could not even imagine how alone and afraid he felt while he lay there and waited for someone to come. I blamed myself for not being by his side when he needed me most. The guilt I felt was nearly unbearable. Jim was taken to the hospital to be examined and returned a few hours later to the nursing home. Although I had provided so much information regarding his health, especially his seizures, this was out of my control. What I had feared the most had happened on Jim's third night, and I was so afraid of what lay ahead. It was a very dark day for me, and I'm sure for him too. Together we had handled the seizures up to this point, and now when he needed me most, I was not there.

BUT HERE WE ARE NOW

In the weeks ahead, there were many more seizures and falls, and each time I felt helpless. I spent more time at the nursing home and did whatever I could to comfort Jim. I needed him to know he wasn't alone, and I wasn't going anywhere. This had been such a big decision to leave our home and enter the nursing facility. Now without the comfort and security of his home, he had to rely on strangers to help him through every need. I know he was scared, but he dug deep into his faith. He never once complained or even spoke of his fear. But he, as always in the past, continued to thank the staff for caring for him and helping to do whatever they could to make him comfortable and safe.

As the seizures and subsequent falls continued, he would be transported to the hospital to ensure he hadn't suffered injuries. Each time, once a blood draw was completed, they would speak of his sky-high white count. They urged him to see an oncologist, and each time Jim refused. As he had stated since last December, he knew the diagnosis and didn't have the fight in him anymore. He had experienced forty years of heart issues, and the last twelve years had proved to be many life-threatening circumstances where he had beaten all the odds. He was simply tired of fighting.

Jim did get to experience some blessings that he had so hoped for in returning to his hometown. So many of our family members, Cabela's friends, co-workers from his time at the high school, hometown friends, and dear friends from his days with the Boy Scouts would pay their visits. One close Scout friend, Gary, would stop by and brighten Jim's day. They would reminisce, and it was such good therapy for Jim. I'm sure everyone who visited never knew how much it meant to him. Once they left, on so many occasions, Jim would have tears in his eyes. Our "comfy quilt" was still warming us both.

Jim got to experience an outing the day before Easter. Byron, Cassie, and Alex took us both downtown for a burger. Jim had told his "favorite nurse" at the nursing home that he would be there that day and she should come by. He said, "I know you probably can't, but I just wanted to invite you anyway." We enjoyed being out for a meal, something we had not done in years. Jim ordered a beer with his burger. He hadn't had one for a few years, and even though they didn't have his favorite MGD— he thoroughly enjoyed it and loved having this time to experience something we hadn't done in forever. The little things in life become the big things for someone in Jim's shoes. To top it all off, as I was pushing Jim in his wheelchair to the car, his "favorite nurse" came running across the parking lot and gave him a big hug. Now his day was complete.

To Jim's delight, our grand fur babies would visit him at the nursing home. Byron and Cassie's dogs, Ammo and Clyde, and Jason's dog, Barney, loved spending time with Jim. To add to the crew, Melissa and Joe brought their fur babies—Dufus, Shadow, and Peanut. The dogs were so special to Jim and brought him such happiness. They would hop up on the bed and lay there, carefully watching Jim in his recliner. If they happened to be there during snack time in the afternoon, they would sit at Jim's feet and hope to get a bite. Jim had a reputation for loving to feed the dogs; the dogs knew it all too well. And as always, he came through and would share his snacks with them. Dogs had always been an important part of Jim's life, and he appreciated it so much that they would bring them for a visit. The other residents in the home loved it as well. The dogs were always such great therapy for Jim, and it brightened his day.

As I mentioned, Jim entered the nursing home on March 11, 2022. On Sunday, June 5, 2022, Jim suffered a serious fall in his room. I had just returned home earlier in the day and received a call that he was being taken by ambulance to the hospital. This fall, unfortunately, did some significant damage. He suffered from a fractured rib and was in excruciating pain. But even more alarming is what the CT scan revealed as well. This test showed that Jim was suffering from lung and kidney cancer. This explained his elevated white count and confirmed our fears. But to make matters even worse, they also discovered an aortic aneurysm—a ticking time bomb. Although the fall caused him so much pain, it did help reveal what Jim was now facing. The medical team knew his condition would quickly deteriorate. Because of this discovery, we met with hospice on Sunday, June 12, and he began services the following day.

Everything seemed to move so quickly. I don't believe we thought this was where we would be now. Just ten days earlier, Jim and I were enjoying coffee together. I would help him onto his motorized scooter, and we would walk on the grounds outside. They had a small pond, and he loved to go over there to see if he could see any ducks. Also, occasionally we would see deer by the edge of the woods, and he would sit there and take it all in. Being outside in nature was one of his greatest pleasures from years ago that we had taken for granted. Each time he could get outside and breathe in the fresh breeze was a blessing. We would sit in his room and watch the birds eat from the feeder I had hung outside his window. He would joke with the staff and have fun teasing everyone. He would sweet-talk the snack coordinator every afternoon to give him an extra banana or pack of Oreos. He would stash the cookies in a drawer for me when I would visit. He was always thinking of others. We would walk through the halls in his scooter, and he would smile and greet the other residents. He especially enjoyed greeting those who were not fortunate to have many visitors. He would brighten their day, as well as his. But ten days later, *here we are now*—in hospice.

When Jim first entered hospice, I was confident he still had months to live on this earth. He now desperately needed extra care, and it was so comforting that it would be provided for him. But shortly after beginning his hospice care, I realized that his health was quickly declining—much more rapidly than anyone had expected. It was soon clear that the many months I thought he had were now quickly turning into days. It was hard to grasp how everything had changed in such a short amount of time. I wasn't ready but I knew I had to be strong for Jim. So here we are now.

Since his fall in early June, I have been going home less and mostly spending time with Jim. With him entering hospice, I remained with him from morning till evening. But by the second week of hospice, Jim had some good days and many not-so-good days. I decided to move into his room to help with his care 24/7. I got to know the St. Croix hospice staff so well, and I am eternally grateful to this day. Until now, I was unfamiliar with the hospice program and what it can provide. I was blown away by all their services and the unending comfort they gave patients and families. They truly are angels on earth. They had joined our "comfy quilt" and gave us both so much love and peace.

I urge anyone going through a severe health issue with their loved one to check out hospice. I was always under the impression that hospice is called in only at the very end. I discovered this is not true. They informed me they have patients who have been with them for months. Even in some instances, patients will "graduate" from hospice and go on to live much longer. But their comfort is immeasurable and shouldn't be denied to anyone who has reached this point in their life. One of the greatest gifts we can give our loved ones near the end is the compassion and comfort that hospice provides to the patient. As a bonus for me, they provided the strength to hold on during when I felt so helpless.

Another hospice service provided was a massage therapist. Sadly, he was drifting in and out the day she came and would begin slumping while sitting in the chair. But the brief massage still had to feel so good to Jim as he was in such pain. Jim was also provided with music therapy, and I have no words to explain how healing that was for both Jim and me. She would visit with her guitar and sing for Jim, asking for his favorite songs. Unfortunately, he was beginning to have many days where he wasn't alert, so Byron, his son, and I would let her know which songs he had always loved. The first time she came was on Tuesday, June 21. She sang one of his favorites for Jim by Johnny Cash—Ring of Fire. For a brief moment, we saw Jim moving his toe to the beat. Although he wasn't alert enough to speak, we knew he could hear and could only imagine how this warmed his heart.

Jim's son, Byron, spent the days with me at Jim's bedside, and I will always be eternally grateful. On one occasion, he asked his friends who owned the downtown café to make a banana cream pie. It was Jim's favorite and Byron wanted to bring him some. They came through and made a delicious pie, and Byron brought a piece to Jim. He had such a smile, and although he could only eat a few bites, I knew he greatly appreciated it. So have a piece of pie for Jim, and don't take it for granted! Take nothing for granted!

Another thing that brought Jim smiles was Harley Davidsons. Years ago, Jim had to give up driving his prized motorcycle. His bike meant the world to him, and it was so difficult when he could no longer ride in confidence. His health prevented him from riding free on the open roads as he had so loved in the past. We had a ritual for many years after he was forced to stop riding. Whenever we were at a stoplight with motorcycles in the next lane, we would roll down the windows so he could hear them drive away. Jim was always known for having loud pipes on his bike and loved listening to a Harley engine revving. If they had quiet pipes, he would shake his head. But if the pipes were loud, he would smile until he couldn't hear them. Jim's two sons each own Harleys, along with Jim's brothers and some dear friends. They would visit Jim in the nursing home, and I only wish they could have seen Jim's face when they left. They would go out to their bikes and rev their engines as they drove off. I had to open the windows so Jim could hear better as they drove away. This simple little gesture brought him so much joy. It helped him to relive his days of announcing his arrivals and departures with his loud Harley pipes! Trust me, back in the day, he never missed an opportunity to make his bike be heard! Never!

Jim and I were fortunate to partake in holy communion with Byron's pastor on three occasions. It meant the world to us to be able to experience this together. Due to Jim's health, we had not been able to physically attend church, other than online services, for so many years. Also, the hospice chaplain would visit and pray with us, providing another layer of comfort. As I mentioned earlier, I genuinely believe that God had woven the pastor and the entire hospice staff into our "comfy quilt." We continued to find warmth and blessing from this "quilt" as we came closer to the end of our journey. Our "quilt" also included a select few from the nursing home who went above and beyond in caring for Jim. One, in particular, was extraordinary and Jim's favorite. I am confident she knows who she is and how special she was to us both.

On June 17, five days after entering hospice, their chaplain and some close family members visited Jim's room for a special ceremony. There is an organization of women who lovingly handcraft quilts for veterans facing their time on earth coming closer to an end. The chaplain brought Jim one of these quilts and had a brief ceremony presenting it to him. He finished with a time of prayer, and tears ran down my face. It was so emotional; my biggest regret was that Jim was unaware of everything. He had slept most of the past twenty-four hours but briefly opened his eyes and gave the chaplain one of his beautiful smiles. Just as quickly as that happened, he was again sleeping. Reality then hit me, and I began to sob. Until now, I had done my best to remain strong for Jim. But now the tears fell uncontrollably, and I was relieved Jim couldn't see my emotions spilling out.

I believed the "comfy quilt" of family and friends that had gotten us to this day was now being bonded with this quilt. God had spoken and given Jim this beautiful, handcrafted quilt to add to our "comfy quilt," we could hear God again whisper, "I've got this." God had brought us this far on an unbelievable journey, and He had not forsaken us now. He was there in this quiet hour to let us both know that He would accompany Jim on the final leg of his journey. In my wildest imagination, I cannot comprehend the warmth and beauty of the heavenly "comfy quilt" that awaited Jim's arrival. As I write this memory, the tears fall, remembering that beautiful day. Later that same day, the nurse came in and had to wake Jim to give him his meds. This was the first Jim had seen the quilt, and I told him that, unfortunately, he had slept through the ceremony. He looked at me and softly said with sadness, "Oh shit," and then immediately went back to sleep. That's my Jim.

So, appreciate the little things—banana cream pie, a motorcycle revving at the stoplight, a beer and a burger, your beloved pets, and a quilt to warm you when you need to feel comfy and loved. These are all gifts that we take for granted. But for Jim, these gifts were priceless.

'I JUST WANT TO GO HOME

We were coming closer to Jim's wish. On days when he could softly speak, he would utter, "I just want to go home." We both knew he didn't mean Blaine but meant his heavenly home. My comfort came in knowing that Jim would not take this final journey alone. God would once again whisper, "I've got this." I knew I would have to let go, and the pain would be unbearable. But I also knew that Jim's earthly pain that he had suffered for so long would now be over. I was so sad for him but so happy as well. He had always paid his dues, never complaining, and I knew he had a home in heaven waiting for him. This God-given peace would be what gave me strength for the days ahead.

On Father's Day, June 19, Jim was blessed with family visits and phone calls. He was exhausted, but between naps, he spent precious time with Byron and Cassie, our dear friends Chy and Don, and my son Travis and granddaughter Declan. He also had a great phone visit with my son, Jason, and daughter, Melissa. Each of these cherished times was so special to Jim. I pray that these visits will forever be treasured memories of his friends and family. He became less alert as the day passed, but these memories will always be present.

I believe one of the hardest things to accept was the first day I didn't get a phone call from Jim. For twenty-two years, I can honestly say there wasn't a single day that we didn't talk. If we were apart in rare times, we would always call one another. When I would leave the nursing home to go to my sons for the night - Jim would always call me at least twice before we went to sleep. And in the mornings, he would always call to say hello before I arrived back at the nursing home. Earlier in his stay at the nursing home, when I would travel back and forth to Blaine, we would talk five or six times a day on the phone. It was just something we always did.

I hadn't received a call for several days, but on Monday, June 20, I got a call from him that evening after I had left for the day. We talked briefly, and he told me he was watching deer outside his window. I returned in the morning and spent the day with him, but he did not call that evening. I tried calling him but got no answer. At 1:30 a.m. in the early morning of June 22, I received a call from Jim. He had been experiencing trouble distinguishing between night and day, and I was sure he thought it was daytime. It lasted only seconds, and he asked where I was. I answered that I would be back in a few hours, and the call ended just like that. I again tried calling him in the morning before leaving for the nursing home. I again got no answer, and from then on, we had no more phone conversations. It may seem like a little thing to some, but it wasn't easy to accept. I knew Jim was slowly slipping away from me, which saddened me. Please take away a lesson from my story…call your loved ones, even just to say hello. You never know when no one will be on the other end of the line.

This week our dear friends, Chy and Don, came to visit and took a photo of Jim and me. This would turn out to be the last picture of us together. Jim had several more visitors and tried his hardest to stay awake and make conversation. He was very sedated from all the pain but did his best. He was never one to complain about his pain levels, no matter how severe. All through the years, he would answer a four or five when asked what his pain level was. He lived with chronic neck and back pain but fought it over the years. I knew he had days where it was much worse, but again, he never complained. After his fall and fractured rib, he bumped his pain level up to a seven, so I knew he was suffering. But later on Wed, June 22, he woke up and asked for more pain meds. I asked his pain level on a scale of one to ten, and he answered, "Eighty-eight!" I knew the pain was more than he could bear, and I felt helpless. I hated seeing him suffer like this and felt so sorry for him. I prayed to God to please ease his pain. We knew Jim's time was fading, but I only wanted his last days to be peaceful and pain-free.

Once I had moved into Jim's room with him 24/7, I would sit in the recliner at the end of his bed. His breathing had become shallower, and during the nighttime hours, I would watch him. I had placed a stuffed animal, a black Harley Davidson dog, on his chest, and I would watch the dog move up and down with each breath. The hospice team had now halted most of Jim's medications, and he was receiving morphine. He was in immense pain and would groan badly when they would turn him on his side to change his pad. Hospice had suspected that he may suffer from bone and possibly brain cancer in addition to lung and kidney cancer. The fractured rib and this possibility were painful for Jim, and his dosages were increased as needed. I remember hating it when it was time for them to turn Jim in his hospice bed again. It brought indescribable pain and tears to both his eyes and mine.

Jim again had visitors on Thursday, June 23, who stopped in to say their goodbyes. He was now sleeping almost nonstop, but he did manage once to open his eyes for Amanda and give her a faint smile. On Friday, June 24, I put a sign on Jim's door celebrating the twelfth anniversary of his heart transplant. Jim was not alert for this day, but I wanted everyone to know of Jim's accomplishment. My brother, Wayne, drove up to visit. For a moment, Jim opened his eyes and faintly smiled at my brother before drifting back into his deep sleep. He thought the world of Wayne and I hoped he realized that Wayne was there for him in these final days. Each of these very brief moments experienced all week by so many visitors meant the world to them and, I'm sure, brought peace to Jim.

I hadn't left his room for days, and on Saturday, June 25, 2022, the staff urged me to go to my son's that evening and get a good night's rest. I resisted over and over, but they finally convinced me. The staff had positioned pillows around Jim to help prevent him from moving. He had tried that day to roll over and even to get out of bed. With his high doses of morphine, this would have been a disaster, plus he couldn't walk alone. I ensured his "pillow wall" was in place, met with the overnight staff, and reluctantly left that evening. I told them to call me for anything—I just needed to know he would be safe.

I did not get a call but found out what happened at 6:30 a.m. the following day when I arrived. I don't know if you are familiar with what they call the last hurrah at the end of life. It is said the patient will attempt to do something their health has robbed them of experiencing. Jim, he had been robbed of walking for so many years. I learned that while he was alone in his room shortly after midnight, he got out of bed and began walking down the hallway! When one of the health assistants saw him walking toward the end of the hall, he said he couldn't believe his eyes. Not only was Jim walking without assistance or a walker, but he said that Jim was walking briskly.

This was Jim's last hurrah. He had been denied walking for so long, and his last wish was to accomplish this task again. Only by God's guiding arm could this have happened. We take walking for granted, but for Jim, it meant the world to him to take one last walk here on Earth. I believe Jim's entire life was led by faith in God, especially in the last twelve years. In Hebrews 12:1 we read, "Therefore we are surrounded by such a great a cloud of witnesses, let us throw off everything that hinders, and the sin that so easily entangles, and let us run with perseverance the race marked out for us." Jim had run the race of life, and now after years of being unable to run or walk for that matter—he got to run one last time with endurance solely by God's help. Jesus allowed this one last walk on earth before Jim would take the final walk to his heavenly home. Jim was graciously allowed this experience, guided by his Lord, and I cannot even imagine how it made him feel. Jim and Jesus alone shared this private moment, and I know it had to bring Jim incredible happiness.

What happened next didn't go as well. Jim was moved in his wheelchair to the area by the nurse's station so they could keep an eye on him. While sitting there, he got up again but couldn't walk and immediately fell to the floor. He was then placed into one of the recliners, where I found him when I arrived early that Sunday morning, June 26.

LAST HURRAH

For months I have beaten myself up for not being there that night. I should have listened to the feeling and stayed with Jim. I knew he was now in even more pain after this last fall, and I felt responsible. After many months of feeling this gut-wrenching guilt, I recently had a thought that changed my outlook on that night. If I had stayed that night with Jim, I would have stopped him from getting out of bed. I would have told him he needed to stay put to stay safe. I now realize that if I had done that, I would have prevented Jim from his last hurrah. He would not have gotten to take that last walk on earth as he so clearly wanted to do. Yes, he wouldn't have suffered the fall—but for Jim, I can only guess that it was the price he was willing to pay to walk one... more... time. Looking back, I believe I was supposed to leave that night so Jim could experience his last earthly walk. He walked his last hurrah with the Lord at his side. Once again, God whispered, "I've got this."

As we got Jim back to his room and into bed, with tears, he whispered, "I want to go home." Jim had gotten his last wish — to take his walk - and was now ready to take the final step. Jim had many family and friends visit during the final few days. Jaqui came and spent the night with me in Jim's room and brought me so much love and support. Hospice added a fentanyl patch, along with morphine, to help with Jim's pain. They were confident the cancer was rapidly spreading and causing him such intense discomfort. On Monday, along with his pain, Jim ran a fever, and his oxygen, blood pressure, and blood sugars wildly fluctuated all day. He once again muttered through the pain the word, "home." This was the last word spoken as he neared the end. Hospice was giving Jim the best possible care as he lay there helpless. They would gently wash his face and put cool washcloths on his forehead. The fever made him sweat, and the cool cloth would briefly relieve him. We also had a fan blowing to help with his comfort. Hospice decided on this day to double the dose of his patch to help relieve Jim of his excruciating pain. Watching him suffer deeply brought me so much sadness, and I prayed to God to please bring him peace.

On Tuesday, June 28, the music therapist once again sang for Jim. He lay motionless in bed and had not communicated since his brief word early yesterday. But when she played and sang for him, he raised his eyebrow briefly during one of the songs. We all took that as a sign that he was still with us and approved the music selections. I still have videos of her playing for Jim as he lay there. They bring tears each time I view them, but they are priceless, and I will forever cherish them. Jim's hospice nurse, Liz, had been coming every day for some time and was my anchor through this journey. We all knew what the outcome would be; getting to the outcome was just painful. She provided Jim and me, along with Bryon, comfort, and peace as we got closer with each passing hour. That evening Jim's son, Leo, and his wife, Shayla, came for a visit. Jim was unresponsive, but I believe in my heart he could hear their voices and knew they were there. It was such a touching moment and one I'll never forget. Pastor Dave had also been by with words of comfort for Jim's final journey.

On Wednesday, June 29, another dear family friend, Josie, and her children came to bring me some clean clothes. Jim was unresponsive, but it was good to have them here for support. Later that same morning, Byron and I discovered that a co-worker of Jim's from Prentice Trucking recently became a resident at the nursing home. I stopped in his room briefly to let him know Jim was just a few doors down. Shortly after, he came down to Jim's room in his wheelchair and said kind words about Jim and their friendship. He said, "I remember the first time I met Jim. When I saw his biceps, I thought to myself...this is someone who you DO NOT want to get in a fight with!" He said Jim was a great friend and would do anything for you. He got that right—Jim had a big heart, and if you treated him with respect—he would move mountains for you if he could. His co-worker felt the need to say these words, and it meant so much to Byron and me.

Our hospice nurse, Liz, visited again this morning and did everything possible to keep Jim comfortable. Jim was now experiencing the "rattle" in his throat, which typically signals death can be only hours away. Soon after she left, Byron went to get us a pizza for lunch. Shortly after he left, the hospice chaplain stopped by for a final blessing. We were talking, and I remember telling him I didn't know how I was going to find my purpose. I had been Jim's caregiver for the past twelve years, and I knew nothing else. This had been my world, and I wouldn't have had it any other way. But now, I was facing a world without Jim, and I didn't know how to navigate my life ahead. It was an extremely emotional visit, and I can honestly say I felt the Holy Spirit in the room. It was something I had never felt before and it was mighty. I was filled with fear but just as much with peace. I can't explain it, but I knew God was with me.

About ten minutes later, Byron came back from downtown with our pizza. He sat down, and as quickly as he had entered the room, the chaplain looked at me and said, "Jim has gone home." At that very moment, it was like Jim had waited until Byron, and I were together so we could lean on one another. Even at his last dying breath, he ensured we would be okay. I threw myself onto Jim's body and sobbed across his chest. I knew he was no longer in pain and abiding in God's presence in heaven. My emotions were all over the place—sadness, relief, grief, and joy. I really couldn't say which emotion was the most powerful. They all were so overwhelming, but reality quickly flooded in, and I couldn't begin to imagine my life without Jim.

THE FINAL CHAPTER

In John 14:1-3 we read, "Do not let your hearts be troubled. Trust in God; believe also in me. In my father's house are many rooms. If it were not so, I would have told you. I am going there to prepare a place for you. And if I go and prepare a place for you, I will come back and take you to be with me so that you also may be where I am." I know in my heart that at Jim's final moment, God was there to bring him on his final walk to his new home. The same home that Jim would speak about when he uttered the words, "I just want to go home." Even though my sadness would sometimes overwhelm me, I had to remember that Jim was now free from his earthly pain and could once again run with his beloved dog, Gunner. I knew I had to focus on this mental picture to get through the grieving I knew was ahead.

Earlier in my book, I referenced the verse from Psalm 32:7. "You are my hiding place. You will protect me from trouble and surround me with songs of deliverance." God had protected Jim all these years through his trouble, and now God was surrounding Jim with His glory and songs of deliverance. Jim's final chapter would be better than all the previous chapters of his life combined. Many of those chapters up to this point were woven with pain and suffering, but now his final chapter would be glorious. As the verse states, we have His protection in times of trouble. But he also offers Himself as our hiding place. Everyone needs a safe space where they can find quiet peace. This verse clarifies that God is offering Himself as our hiding place. We need to recognize when we need that space to keep going. God will always be there waiting. It is free for the asking; the price was paid on the cross. So, I encourage you to seek His hiding place when you feel alone and need the comfort of His arms. There is no punch card on how many times you can visit. He will be there, whether it is only occasionally or several times a day.

To this day, I find myself struggling with the fact that God allowed me to beat cancer. I am beyond and forever grateful, but it comes with a high cost of guilt. This horrible and relentless disease took the life of Jim, my brother, my brother-in-law, and lately so many dear friends. I will always feel guilty when someone else fights the fight but is not allowed to win. But thankfully their prize is waiting for them in heaven. To honor them, we must remain focused on letting our light shine for others while on this earth. But I must confess, I am jealous of the peace that Jim is now feeling. We live in a troubled world with sin and sadness everywhere. What brings me peace is knowing Jim's peace and we will meet again. Now back to Psalm 32:7. This passage was the bible verse in my morning devotions on June 29, 2022. I read this verse only four hours before Jim's passing.

From the moment of Jim's death, I saw signs of Jim sending a subtle message that both he and God were watching over me. I called these signs Godwinks. Eleven books have been written regarding Godwinks by Squire Rushnell, and I encourage you to read them. We have signs everywhere that are sent to us, but we so many times miss the signs. Either we are too busy or distracted or don't believe in them. Some may call these coincidences, which is fine; everyone has a right to an opinion. I, however, believe these are signs from heaven letting us know we aren't alone. I witnessed these signs both the evening of Jim's passing and one week later the evening of his funeral. My son's lake home has sunsets that are both mesmerizing and beautiful. Sunsets have always been a favorite of mine and I love taking their photos. God paints a new one every night; it is a shame if we don't notice and thank Him for the beauty. But both evenings, it was the most spectacular sunset I have ever seen. The cover photo of my book was Jim's final sunset from the night of his funeral.

Pastor Dave officiated Jim's funeral at his small country church, just like I knew Jim would want. The service was amazing and a great tribute to Jim. Afterward, while everyone was outside during the playing of taps, an eagle soared above in the skies. To me, this was definitely a Godwink. It was as if Jim was flying overhead, saying he was watching over us. I also believe he was flying overhead to hear a sound that he so loved one more time. Many of his family and friends drove their motorcycles to the funeral in honor of Jim. After the flag ceremony, many bike owners started their Harleys and revved their engines. I can only imagine the smile this brought to Jim. I wanted to get this on a video to remember, but I didn't have my phone. My friend, Jaqui, ran into the church to get my cell phone. She returned to the parking lot and asked Jim's nephew, Tim if he would start his bike up again for one final revving. He graciously did this, and I recorded it just for Jim. They had always shared a close bond, and now he could pay tribute to his beloved uncle. To this day, I still play the video as a sweet memory in honor of Jim.

My other never failing Godwink is my cardinal. Since Jim's passing, there has not been a single day that my red cardinal hasn't visited me. Some say that cardinals signify that someone in heaven is thinking about us. I hold onto that belief because it helps me process my grief and loss. I spend many hours in the living room, drinking coffee and watching out onto the deck, waiting for my cardinal. Now with warmer weather, I can enjoy my coffee outside on the deck with my cardinal. There have been days when I am distracted and am not looking out the window. If this happens during his visit, my cardinal will begin to sing, and I know he is saying, "Hellooooo??!!" This has happened way too many times to be a coincidence. For me, it's my Godwink.

The dictionary definition for Godwink is as follows: An event or personal experience, often identified as coincidence. So astonishing that it is seen as a sign of divine intervention, especially when perceived as the answer to a prayer. As I said earlier, everyone has the right to their own opinion, and I believe these signs are Godwinks. It helps me throughout my day and has now become a mission of mine to find these Godwinks. The more we slow down and look for God, the more we find his subtle messages. I believe this is God's gentle nudge letting us know we aren't alone in this world.

Jim's final chapter brought him so much suffering. But he is now at peace. My faith, my "comfy quilt" of family and friends, and my Godwinks have brought me to this day and to my peace. I know that one day I will be reunited with Jim and my family members, who have also made the journey to heaven.

This one fact is what keeps me going even when times get tough. We never have to walk this journey on Earth alone.

I want to sincerely thank you for purchasing and reading my book. My sincere hope and my goal in writing this is that I may touch even just one life to find hope for their journey. We will face both good and bad times throughout our life. We do not get to choose the ending, but we do get to walk it with God. I have repeatedly learned that each chapter in our life strengthens us. Each struggle brings an even deeper strength to our souls. These strengths are layered one on top of another with each struggle we face. As our journey in life progresses, each layer of strength brings us one step closer to God and further deepens our faith.

Looking back over life, I believe our struggles have been meant to prepare us for our final journey. They have not been a punishment—I would believe they are a test. Each struggle we face can show God that because of his sacrifice on the cross, we can also face our struggles by leaning on our faith. He is always there to walk beside us; we just have to ask. It is really that simple. I am ready for this final journey whenever God calls my name. Until then, I will face the good and the bad, knowing I am not alone.

THE FINAL FINAL CHAPTER

Whether we are in good times or bad—we always get to choose whether to walk with God or to walk alone.

If we slow down and listen, God whispers ever so gently, "I've got this."

And finally, to Jim—thank you for sharing your light with others whenever darkness surrounded you. You were an inspiration, and provided unending hope, to so many who shared your journey. As you soar with the angels, know that you are loved and missed. Until we meet again.